Adaọra's Adulting Chronicles

A Journal Novella about Growing Up

Adaora's Adulting Chronicles

Adaora's Adulting Chronicles

A Journal Novella about Growing Up

A record of this book is available from the British Library.

Paperback ISBN: 978-1-0687144-6-7
Hardback ISBN: 978-1-0687144-7-4
e-book ISBN: 978-1-0687144-8-1

Publisher: Authentic Worth
Website: www.authenticworth.com

Adaora's Adulting Chronicles

Table of Contents

Acknowledgements

To my Father in Heaven, God; Teacher, Lord, Friend, and Giver of Good Gifts; thank you. For the opportunity and grace to steward this gift, and to do it, well. Thank You for your patience with me; it took me a minute to get over me, and here we are. All glory and honour to Your Name, forever. May your sacrifice, Jesus, not be in vain in my life; Amen.

To my Mama, *Ngozi (aka Ngo baby),* who saw and nurtured this gift even before I knew it was a gift; thank you. Your love for literature spurred me. The countless books you bought me, inspired me, and your constant validation of my writing (and really, all that I do) since inception, encouraged me and (still does). I love you SO much!

To my Papa, *Chief Oliver,* one of whose many prayers for me was that "God shines my light, so that I will be a model in the family in Imo State Nigeria, in the UK and the world at large through Christ our Lord." Thank you. I pray that this is another brick to the actualisation of that prayer. Also, thank you for being so particular about my writing and handwriting – for always marking up a lot of my writings when I was younger, for grammar and spelling with detailed feedback. All of which, now, symbolise your encouragement for me to write and exercise creativity well. I guess you could say that it paid off? I love you Popsy!

To my Mama Onyinye and Papa Charles; thank you so much for all your sacrifices that have catapulted and led to an array of opportunities and becoming, including this one. It does not go unnoticed - may God continue to reward you for everything. I appreciate you so!

To my Uncle Uche, Uncle Emma and Aunty Justina, who were constant and avid readers of my blogs when it first launched. I'm not sure you know what every comment you left did for me. Thank you for your support, and to everyone else who supported my blog when it launched; THANK YOU!

To my sister, my first editor, my sounding board on many occasions, Chisom; thank you. Words will not be enough. Thank you for always being willing to read and give me feedback, suggestions, and support. Thank you for penning such a fantastic and heartfelt foreword. You are so amazing. We did it boo! I love you soooo much!

To my friend, Stephen, who believed in me when I first pitched this idea of writing a book. You believed with no iota of doubt; it was a little shocking! But then again, that's what you do – even if I wanted to run for President tomorrow, you'd support me because that's just you. Thank you, friend.

To my friend, Audrey; your ability to chase after your own dreams and steward your gifts well, was and is inspiring to me. Thank you for holding me accountable, for your feedback and believing in this book. Thank you for being one of my biggest cheerleaders and for championing this project as though it was yours. Your love and support are so palpable.

To my friend, Denise. Your pride, excitement and admiration for the actualisation of my dreams and what were once prayer requests, is beautiful and anchoring. Thank you for your prayers & support, friend!

To Kika, whose life and ministry has blessed me by the grace of God in ways I cannot begin to explain. Dare I say, even changed the trajectory of my life; thank you. Your yes is not wasted. What God said through you was the "go ahead" I needed. Thank you, and I cannot wait for us both to testify – "See what the Lord has done!" not only in my life, but in yours and in the lives of all He has used you to impact.

To everyone, and I mean everyone who has validated my writing – my wider circle of family and friends, RCCG POJ Chelmsford community, Team Obedience family, everyone that has commented, DM'ed me, shared, engaged, encouraged, and supported in whatever capacity; thank you. All of this has contributed and led me up to this point. I appreciate you all SO much.

To *The Writers Club (@the.writers.clb)*; a necessary space for writers; thank you. The space encouraged me. Being surrounded by amazing writers who were able to give me feedback, spurred me on the more and provided a necessary community for writing which can be lonely at times.

To everyone who read various iterations of this book: Chisom, Stephen, Audrey, Jas, Funso, Nsuaha – THANK YOU! Your support and feedback were invaluable.

Nsuaha, thank you for taking accountability to another level. For championing my dreams as though they were yours. For literally taking it upon yourself to make sure that I see them to the very end, brick by brick

– man, thank you so much. If this isn't love, then I don't know what is? Hehe. I love you.

To my Publisher, Esther and the Authentic Worth Team, **thank you** for holding my hand through this process. The book would definitely not have been birthed without everything you poured into this project. Thank you for your patience with me, your accommodation, encouragement and for getting behind this vision with so much optimism and excitement. God bless you all a million times.

To everyone in my life who are parts of Adaọra and mirror her experiences; thank you – I hope you know that your journey is not in vain and that you are not alone.

To every reader who might relate with Adaọra, I hope you feel seen and know that you're not alone. May Adaọra's journey be a reminder for you to give yourself grace on your journey, too.

Finally, to every creative in whatever capacity, you all inspire me – thank you!

Foreword

It is with immense joy and pride that I pen this foreword for my sister, Adaeze, on her debut book "Adaọra's Adulting Chronicles." A beautifully crafted gift to readers, offering an intimate and relatable account of a journey through the exhilarating, confusing, and often-comical realities of adulthood. From the outset, her writing is both refreshing, insightful, and often funny, making this book a true pleasure to read.

Her compilation of personal essays and reflections stands as a testament to Adaọra's journey of self-discovery and growth through the often-turbulent waters of adulthood. She doesn't shy away from sharing the challenges she's faced, whether it's grappling with the complexities of her unconventional family, cross-cultural experiences, the intricacies of friendships, grief, trauma, identity crisis or confronting the societal and cultural expectations placed upon her as a young Nigerian woman. She invites us into her coming of age, allowing us to witness her moments of vulnerability, her hard-won triumphs, and the valuable lessons she's learned along the way.

Through candid storytelling and heartfelt reflections, Adaọra provides a relatable and honest look at the universal experiences that shape our world. This book is more than just a journal novella; it's an invitation to embrace the messy, beautiful, and often-unpredictable nature of adulting. It's a celebration of the human experience -- a reminder that none of us are alone in our struggles, and that through shared experiences and honest conversations, we can find comfort, support, and even a touch of humour in the midst of life's challenges.

As you turn the pages of this book, I encourage you to reflect on your own journey, to find resonance with Adaọra's experiences, and embrace the transformative power of self-reflection and growth. Let Adaọra's words be the lens for you to feel seen; a catalyst for your own personal exploration, and may her story empower you to navigate the complexities of adulting with patience, courage, authenticity, and a renewed sense of hope, *Oga di mma.*

With love,

Chisom Mbata.

Adaora's Adulting Chronicles

Prologue

Mama taught me to put my words to paper. As an extremely reserved child, she thought it was wise for me to learn how to process my thoughts and create room as a way to acknowledge the many feelings and complexities in my mind that I struggled a lot of times to vocally express. At the time, I did not fully grasp what she did for me, but now I do.

So, here I am, following mama's prompts, particularly in my attempt to try and process this whirlwind that is *adulting*. I feel like I am in the peak of it, yet, I am sure that this is in fact, only the beginning.

I don't exactly know what this is – a journal? A collection of notes? A long rant? A collection of reflections?

I'm not sure…

In many ways, it juxtaposes my experience of adulting thus far – daunting, unclear, and a whole lot of processing sprinkled with the need for patience and grace.

Adaora's Adulting Chronicles

A Scam!

"Grow up!" they said.

"Adulting is a scam!" – a phrase that I have repeated to myself countless of times over. It became more frequent and apparent once I graduated from university and was welcomed by the hands of the "real world." Same world, I was conditioned to look forward to in some sense. I cannot exactly pinpoint who or what did the conditioning, and I am not exactly sure what I was expecting it to look or be like, however, this complexity was not in the picture.

It is not as linear as I thought it would be…

I got bored one day and in a spur of the moment, decided to look up the definition of adulting. Perhaps, this was one of my many moments of trying to make sense of it all. I was not shocked at all to find out the dictionary's meaning is not as clear as I had hoped:

Adulting – *"the practice of behaving in a way characteristic of a responsible adult, especially the accomplishment of mundane but necessary tasks." (A definition according to the Oxford dictionary).*

I guess from that definition and my experience so far, it simply means to **take responsibility of…** In this case, yourself – which is very nuanced.

I looked forward to adulthood when I was younger. I was so caught up with the idea of growing up. I believe this strong desire stemmed from the fact that I perhaps interpreted "adulthood" as "freedom." Maybe that was how it was portrayed to me?

"When I am older, I'll be free to do what I want!", "No one can tell me what to do" or better still, *"I just need to grow up and live my life!"* My naïve self would ponder on these thoughts from time to time, filled with so much excitement about what the future holds.

In a sense, I was not completely wrong. The older I became, the more independent I turned out to be and, in that regard, my "freedom" increased – freedom to make decisions for myself, to think for myself.

However, this was not as easy as it sounded, sometimes. Most times, even.

I wish I was privy to some rea-li-ties of adulting before I started to become one. But then again, is there really a manual to adulting? There is no blueprint per se.

I agree with the train of thought that likens adulting to parenting – in a lot of ways, they are similar. It is something one has to experience and learn from. Adulting must be experienced to be understood, I think.

The older I got, most of my conversations with some of my friends have revolved around adulting. We bonded over the fact that most of us felt a bit unprepared for it. We know there is no manual, but can we get a manual?!

The journey so far has felt constant; there's always something – something to learn, to unlearn, to grieve, to grow from or grow through or into, to do, to navigate…the list goes on.

If only my younger self knew that I was in for a ride…

PART I

How did we get here?

1.

Connecting the Dots: Family & Upbringing

My family is a little unconventional. Papa, my father, and my mother (mama) were university sweethearts. They met at a social event at Abia State University – a state government-owned and operated Nigerian university, located at the eastern part of the country. At the time, Papa was in his final year studying Accounting, and mama was in her penultimate year. She studied English Language and Literature.

"It was interest at first sight," I recall mama saying when I asked her about how her and papa met.

(Papa: tall, fashionable, charismatic, cool and witty. Mama: beautiful, sensitive, hardworking, empathetic, resilient).

This interest grew because Papa had (still has) such a charisma – he is very personable, lighting up every room he walks into. He is funny. Mama loved that about him and that was what caught her interest in him. Fast forward a couple of months later, they both started dating. Courting, should I say.

"Things were different in our days. "Ụwa emebiela ugbu a*", mama said to me in our conversation [meaning the world has spoilt now]. We had been discussing dating in this context. In their days, it seemed much straightforward. More intentional; man meets woman, both liked each other and had similar values, both made a commitment to each other, and this started their journey to marriage: courtship being the first step. Easy… or so it seemed.

After graduation, Papa started his own small business. He had a warehouse where he traded groceries; importing and exporting inter-state. Papa had always been a go-getter. He was not from the wealthiest of families, was the first offspring of three children, which meant he had such a huge responsibility from an early age. This fast tracked his journey to maturity. A tale of an average Nigerian.

Papa's father (Pa Tobias), my granddad, was a farmer. He owned a few palm plantations where he made a decent amount of money from his produce which he used to train up Papa to university level. Culturally, education is seen as the best gift parents could leave for their children; a purveyor of opportunities. Therefore, my granddad did all he could to put papa through school.

After school, Papa, then immediately had to take on the baton from his father to support the family and the rest of his siblings financially. Something he carried on doing for as long as he could, even when he eventually had a family of his own. Papa is industrious – that could be a testament to the fact that he is Igbo or the fact that he had to 'hustle' from an early age or both but, he sure was and still is.

Once mama graduated, they both got married. They married young. The early stages of their marriage according to mama's tales, was sweet – they were young and in love. It was filled with so much laughter, love, and joy. They were both friends so it felt seamless.

And then life hit…

Five years into their union, mama was still struggling to conceive – miscarriage after miscarriage after miscarriage; about six in total. It was devastating and unsurprisingly I guess, that put a strain on their union.

Unfortunately, the culture was not kind to mama during that experience. It isn't to women like her. Mama was blamed for her inability to conceive. Motherhood was often the only way for a woman to stabilise her position in the community and the family of her husband. Children tend to offer an "assurance of both personal immortality and old age insurance"[1] (from the perspective of their cultures which traditionally had a patriarchal structure) and mama, was yet to have one. She faced so much social stigma, even from her own husband's family.

"She must be cursed!"

"Why can't she carry a child of her own? Who knows what she did when she was younger?"

"She needs prayers!"

"She must be a man!"

"Her husband should just marry another wife!"

These were some of the comments mama received – some directly and others she overheard people say. She was even taken to many 'prayer houses' for some type of *intervention*. It was a lot – traumatic is the word. Till this day, I marvel at how she has overcome all of this.

Four additional years later after her last miscarriage, mama conceived.

I was the fruit!

Mama adores me and I her. We have a beautiful relationship. It was just me at the time, and so I found a friend in her growing up. We played games together; she always indulged me. She was a disciplinarian in her own way, but I could count the number of times she raised her hand on me as a form of discipline – it was almost non-existent. My childhood friends marvelled at my experiences each time I told them about this - for a lot of Nigerians, discipline looked like getting a whip or beating in the name of 'correction.' My experience was quite different – I only experienced that at school.

Growing up, I could tell Papa adored me too. Whatever I wanted, he got for me – I remember him always buying me snacks or takeaway foods; Mr Biggs was my favourite. On the days he didn't buy anything, I'd be so upset (that's how spoilt I was!)

"I'm sorry, work was busy, but I'll get you something tomorrow," he would always say to reassure me on said days.

Papa drove me to school and back. He ironed my uniform most of the time – his ironing was so crisp! (He should have started a dry-cleaning company I think). Although I knew Papa adored me, I feared him. He was sometimes a little irritable and when he was upset, he expressed them through words that were not so pleasant. His words stung; they stung more to me and most times, I wished he had hit me instead.

But I knew he loved me. The older I got, the dynamics of our relationship fluctuated and his *next significant* move was devastating to me.

Eventually, he succumbed to *"her husband should just marry another wife"* suggestions – especially when this was echoed by pretty much his entire family…

I'm not sure what happened or what changed, but I noticed that he grew to tolerate mama as a result. It's interesting sometimes how parents don't realise how much their children notice or pick up even at a such a young age. Papa somewhat started to treat mama as a second-class citizen (some days, I felt he loved me more than he did his wife). I saw it. It bothered me, but I did not know what to do about it.

I guess the pressure was too much on him as well. Or maybe he felt so guilty about marrying this second wife so pushing mama away was a defence mechanism, perhaps.

Although, I had come along and that was beautiful, mama didn't have any more children and…I wasn't a boy anyway, so most people thought papa's move was "wise" and in fact, instigated it. Again, blame patriarchy?

I could tell Papa's move crushed mama. His actions communicated and echoed her 'inadequacy.' That her own husband thought she wasn't enough.

Aunty* Adaego, was an embodiment of her name – she was born into wealth.

She was from a wealthy family, from Anambra State in Nigeria. She was introduced to Papa by a family friend before they got married.

Aunty Adaego had an interesting life too. Born to a white British mother and a black Nigerian father in the United Kingdom. However, her mother and father separated when she was only 3 years old. She was basically raised by her father. Although she was a British, she was very much Nigerian.

When she was 12, Adaego's father relocated back to Lagos, Nigeria. She went to a private secondary school in Nigeria, travelled back to the UK to attend University and returned to Nigeria again to complete her NYSC on her father's request after she graduated.

NYSC, the **N**ational **Y**outh **S**ervice **C**orps is a national programme set up by the Nigerian government (during the military regime) in a bid to reconstruct and rebuild the country after the Nigerian Civil War, by encouraging Nigeran graduates to participate in this mandatory one-year programme.

During this programme, members are posted to different states in the country and will undertake various work experiences as well as other experiences which involve physical training, drills, lectures, skill acquisition training, social activities etc. All of which is aimed to create opportunities for the members and foster unity in graduates.

In my opinion, it sounds fancier than it seems as there has been quite a few valid criticisms around the programme. However, I know a few people who enjoyed their experiences (at least the ones who were privileged enough to be sent to an area where sanitary does not become a luxury).

It was during Aunty Adaego's NYSC, that she was introduced to Papa. And the rest as they say, is history.

My father now had a second wife and I was not sure how to feel. Having her around felt a bit weird. We were civil but that was about it. From time to time, my mind pondered on how mama was feeling. I engaged her on the situation as often as I could. As always, she was resilient through it all, but I could tell that she was barely trying to keep it all together, because of me.

Eventually, Aunty Adaego had a child for my father and as destiny would have it, it was a boy – Jide. I was 10 when Jide was born.

The family was ecstatic by his arrival. *"Finally, an heir to Papa's lineage!"*

I sometimes wonder what would have happened if Jide turned out to be a girl – it would have been a little comical in retrospect.

Culture has been simply defined as a people's way of life; encompassing their belief systems, social behaviours, values, customs, traditions (customs transferred from generation to generation), music, food, arts, etc. All of which can evolve over time.

In Igbo tradition, the male child is very important. It is a representation of the family's strength and manhood. A symbol of hope for the continuity of the family lineage, unlike the female child who would eventually be married and take on another surname. I once read an article that echoed the traditional significance of the male child. It says:

"Any family without a male child is seen to have gone into extinction." [6]

I chuckled to myself when I read that – it was a bit of a melodramatic statement if you ask me!

"*Surely, the validity of one's lineage is in more than just the fact that the surname is changed due to marriage. Just because I will get married one day does not make me any less of my father's fruit",* I thought to myself. Anyway, what do I know.

I understand the sentiment that there is power in a name and the belief that ones' name somewhat carries them into their destiny. However, I don't think that it applies to a change in surname because of marriage.

It took me a while to process my feelings towards Aunty Adaego and Jide's arrival. A part of me tried to make sense of it all. Another part of me felt somewhat not good enough and the latter, just felt sorry for mama and wanted to be strong for her too.

Mama carried me through this change. She would try to reassure me at every opportunity she got – *"nne, ọ ga adịnma** {"daughter, it will be well"} was her go-to phrase.

Sometimes, I wondered how she did it; always putting others before herself.

How did she constantly have the courage to keep going despite all that she had been through? How did she not look like what she had been through, even till this day? It can only be God.

Mama's resilience to me, was one of the first testaments to me, that there is a God and He carries us through life's ebbs and flows.

When I was 15, Aunty Adaego decided to relocate back to the UK with Jide.

Not long after, I had to join them. A decision in retrospect that I was not fully prepared for.

2.

Was *japa* a Bad Idea?

In a nutshell, *japa** is a Nigerian buzzword for emigration.

From time to time, the thought of travelling abroad crossed my mind growing up.

From a young age, I had an impression of "abroad" to equate "the land flowing with milk and honey." Milk and honey being synonymous to better opportunities, access to better healthcare, good roads, 24/7 electricity supply and other necessities which have been stifled from the average Nigerian due to bad governance and the lack of systems that work in Nigeria. Not just that, seeing some family friends and relatives on their return from abroad with skin fresher than they left solidified this thought for me.

From a very young age, I was acquainted with this narrative that as an average Nigerian, if the opportunity arose, I had to leave the country to have a good opportunity to thrive. There was this not-so-subtle conviction that things were much better abroad even though I had never been. I was still so young to fully understand or even explore the implications of this.

I didn't see *japa* happening any time soon. So, although I would have these thoughts from time to time, I quickly moved on from them. Little did I know that my own japa journey was much sooner than I anticipated!

I truly believe that if we had better systems in Nigeria, japa would not even be a thing.

Nigeria is home and, home is rich, in every sense of the word.

I grew up in Owerri, a city located in Imo State (the eastern part of Nigeria). We lived in Owerri Municipal – the state's heart. A city made up of three local government areas: Owerri West, Owerri North and Owerri Municipal.

Living in Owerri was great; it was a city that welcomed strangers, loved music and loved a good life – one that was ushered by culture like the Oru Owerri festival*, distinct foods, merriment, and entertainment! This love for merriment and entertainment in the city was also evidenced by the very many bars, restaurants and hotels present in the city.

Igbo people are known to be industrious, and the people of Owerri are no different. The city is filled with lots of markets, some of which were named after the former ezes* (kings) of the local governments within the state.

I attended a Catholic Nursery, Primary and Junior Secondary School. Growing up in a Catholic Christian home, this was non-negotiable. For starters, it was a private school which in many ways meant better quality of education. In addition to that, my parents believed because it was a *Christian* school, moral standards will be much higher. Although that was arguable from my experience, I did get their logic and appreciated my time at those schools.

Mama and Papa did great – for the average Nigerian parent, sending your kids to private schools was no small feat and I am grateful for the sacrifices they made in sending me to one of the best private schools in the area.

My time at the schools were okay. Some random memories come to mind like being so anxious to go to nursery and crying when I arrived at the school gate; there is a standing joke of how mama had to follow me into classrooms to sit with me and then sneak out when I was not looking. Mama made meals for me to take to school for myself and my friends.

Mama and papa gave me pocket money. I was a teacher's pet doing very well academically and being recognised for it. Papa took me to and from school most days (drives consisting of Papa playing his favourite jams in the car and singing passionately to them, but immediately switching to hurl insults at a reckless driver on the road; driving in Nigeria can be an extreme sport sometimes!) Papa ironed my uniforms for school – this is something I still miss; again, my uniforms used to be so crisp! He was really good at it.

I was almost 16 when I had to join Aunty Adaego and Jide in the UK. I had just finished my Junior Secondary School in Nigeria and taken my WAEC* exams which were quite major. The Junior WAEC exams were a compulsory internal examination set by the West African Examinations Council who awards certificates which are comparable to the equivalents of international examining authorities to screen students on different subjects before they transition to senior secondary classes. [8]

Prior to when I had to relocate, arrangements had been made to visit the UK for holiday. It was fun and I loved it.

Although, both papa and mama saw the benefit of me permanently relocating abroad, they were a bit apprehensive for me to relocate to the UK. Rightly so! Their only daughter was moving miles away from them at such a young age but for the 'greater good.'

"If only things were so much better in Nigeria. If only our government and people in places of authority were not consumed by greed, perhaps we would have better systems that work for the average Nigerian", mama lamented in a conversation.

Although I was not necessarily going to be alone, this move was still a big change for my parents. It was, and still is, for me too.

A side note that I did not pick up until later: unfortunately, within the first year of Papa and Aunty Adaego's union, they seemed to run into a hiccup. I know now that I am older, Aunty Adaego felt thrown into the union with my father, by her own father. She had always dreamed of marrying a man who loved her for who she is and not as she would later express in one of her outbursts in the future to me; "a man who sees her as a project."

It was a lot of getting used to my new family dynamic. I was homesick a lot. I missed the bond mama and I shared. It was not the same here.

Although, I am grateful for being abroad and the opportunities that come with it, I sometimes wonder whether it was a good idea.

In hindsight, I think about the neglect I felt growing up because mama was no longer present. In many ways, I had to grow up quickly and parent myself. Aunty Adaego was always working to pay bills so she was never present. Even when she was physically present, she was never…present for me. Perhaps she was just consumed by her new reality; preoccupied with distracting work and trying to make ends meet.

I began to resent her and everything around me because I felt so neglected. I missed mama's friendship so much. I also began to resent Jide too. It felt as though we were both in the same environment, but had different experiences. Aunty Adaego was more sensitive to his needs and a bit more present for him. Perhaps it was because he was her son, and she had a bond with him? Or perhaps she also resented my father and projected that unto me hence the lack of bond. I wasn't sure, but what I was sure about was that she acted different with me.

Her conversations with me were either superficial like the 'have you eaten-type' conversations or the 'you-need-to-do-x-y-z' type of conversations. Other times, they were flat out rants, nagging or what felt like a verbal dumping of general issues or concerns on me. She was also irritable a lot of the times which manifested as shouting or saying hurtful things when she was upset which she never usually apologised for. It was during one of those moments that she expressed her regret of succumbing to her father's pressure of marrying "a man who sees her as a project."

It felt like there was never an intentional or emotional check-in of how I was really doing – really and truly from her. Unlike mama, she didn't check in with what was happening with me, with school, how I was coping, who my friends were…just things that mattered to me. I was quite a sensitive child and it was painful to no longer have that maternal emotional engagement I once had.

My young mind could not comprehend the potential motivations behind her actions like the fact that the status quo in this new country of ours was to work to pay numerous bills which can be an exhausting cycle, and so perhaps she was stressed. I couldn't comprehend that she too, probably had her own struggles navigating being separated from her husband with two kids as well, or this new reality that she probably didn't imagine for herself, and all the other things that came with her being an adult. I couldn't understand that she was a human that needed grace too.

I couldn't understand it. How could I? I was a child. Not just a child, but a child whom things were not communicated to.

The older I got, the more I realised how the move at such a young age and the initial experiences that came with it negatively impacted me in different ways. Ways which showed up in some behavioural patterns as an adult – issues with low self-esteem, self-doubt, internalising my emotions, being unable to be vulnerable, poor boundaries, poor social skills, difficulty in asking for or receiving help, trust issues, negative self-talk, and the increased likelihood of becoming socially isolated or withdrawn.

Another *japa* surprise for me:

I did not realise I was black until I moved abroad!

As insane as it sounds, it is the truth. Growing up back home, my colour was not really something I paid attention to.

Culture? Yes, I knew that was a thing. I was from one of the very many tribes in Nigeria. I had friends who were from different tribes to mine but…we were the same, regardless. We were Nigerians. My blackness, on the other hand, was never really something that stood out to me, until I moved.

The shock that came with this realisation was real.

At my first school at the time, in the rural town of Lincolnshire, I was the only black girl in the entire school. The **entire** school?! That was shocking to me. We had four black teachers and I had never been so grateful for representation when I saw them. Although, as teachers they were much older than me and therefore, I could only relate to them so much. I was just so grateful to see people who looked like me.

My first day at school was terrifying. Staring eyes followed me as I walked into the assembly hall.

I wasn't quite sure what the stare was for. Was it because I was late to school that day? Did I look weird? Had they not seen a black girl before? Or was it a combination of these reasons?

I hurriedly made my way and sat down at the nearest spot I could find as hindsight would reveal with the Year 7s. I was not supposed to sit there but I could not make it to the benches at the back where I was supposed to sit as my anxiety that day wouldn't let me.

My time at that school was interesting. In the first couple of months, I was bombarded with a lot of questions and comments from curious students about me:

"Oh, you're from Africa?"

"You speak really good English!"

"Do you live on trees in Africa?"

"Have you seen lions/zebras/elephants?" "Do you ride on them?"

I wasn't sure how to take all the questions and general curiosity and was taken aback. Confused, I wondered where they had got these narratives from. I mean, I had never seen a zebra in my life. I had never even been to the zoo at the time, let alone use these animals as a mode of transportation as they had questioned! Also, any knowledge I had was limited to Nigeria, not Africa as a whole.

"You should have said yes when you were asked if people lived on trees in Africa. You should have added that when the (late) Queen visited Nigeria in the 50s, we gave her the tallest tree to live on", Mr Abam remarked sarcastically.

Mr Abam was one of the four black teachers in the school. He was my chemistry teacher and was originally from Ghana. His tall, dark frame encompassed so much wit, authenticity, intelligence, and assertiveness. I really liked him. This response was following on from his usual check in with me to see how I was adjusting in the school. I had expressed to him my confusion at some of the questions and comments thus, his hilarious response. It was his way of echoing how ridiculous some of these questions were and I understood it perfectly.

Although, some of the comments and questions I received were not birthed from a place of malicious intent, it was still baffling to hear.

Remaining on the topic of bafflement, another *japa* surprise for me:

The fact that teachers or people in places of authority and responsibility at school (and generally) were referred to by their first names with no prefix.

I struggled to get used to this in the first couple of months at school. I couldn't bring myself to address my teachers *just* by their first names. It was foreign to me. Where I was from, you dared not.

It was seen as disrespectful.

Culturally, referring to someone older than you or in a place of authority by their first name, was a no. There was always a prefix before the name – "aunty/uncle [insert name]" [a common one used even though the person might not necessarily be related to you]. Or just "Sir/Ma" was used to address the person instead.

I could tell it made my teachers uncomfortable when I referred to them as "aunty [X]" or "uncle [Y]." They were so confused by it. Some of them sternly asked me to refrain from that. I then deferred to using "sir "and "ma" but that seemed equally as uncomfortable. It took me a while, but I eventually adapted to just addressing them by their name. A not-so-minute example of the conundrum of continuous adaptations that will ensue.

It seemed like students here generally had a voice. They had the liberty to challenge things when they felt uncomfortable. Granted, some of them took it too far by being rude at times. I wasn't used to this level of liberty in a general sense, but I admired it. Where I was from, yes children had a voice; however, 'culture' meant that sometimes, there was not much freedom or space to express how one genuinely felt without the fear of how it would be perceived. Compliance a lot of times echoed respect. Thus, a lack thereof, disrespect. I was shocked at the sheer audacity that most of the students in my new school had, regardless of whether it was rude or not. In some ways, I aspired to be that audacious; to express how I felt just as they did with less care.

My first school was interesting. Asides the culture shock, there were a few other experiences which also come to mind:

Being bullied was one of them. I was called a "wet dog" on several occasions. I remember instances in my maths class where the girl who sat next to me would pull out her deodorant and spray it in my face. I remember the first time this happened vividly. Some students who caught the act in real time literally gasped. Mouths opened wide communicating the utter shock they were in including myself, but no one said anything. Not even me…

It happened a few times – too many times that I went to the restroom to bawl my eyes out. I already felt like a minority and an outcast: a feeling in which the colour of my skin made me automatically an expert. This bullying exacerbated this. My esteem was on the floor by this point. Eventually, I reported these incidents and it got to the head teacher's office; the perpetrators were cautioned.

Although, I was grateful for the caution, it felt like the damage had already been done.

I struggled to make friends here too. This was an ironic shocker. For someone who came from an environment where she was well-known for her academic prowess, which attracted much popularity and therefore many "friends," this was bewildering. I floated around friendship groups. I was invited to join a popular friendship group in my year at the time, and the school's IT girls were a part of it.

Although that gave me a sense of validation at the time, it was still awkward being a part of that group – my difference was not celebrated nor embraced, and so I felt even more alone.

We (Aunty Adaego, Jide and myself) moved around a lot and that didn't help either. It did not help my struggle with making friends and adapting. Moving around meant that I had to change schools every year; three times since my first school abroad. Without realising, I became accustomed to instability which then had a further ripple effect on me socially.

Although I longed to be in a friendship group, with each new school that followed the first, came a sense of apathy, apprehension, and fear – what was the point of making friends when I might need to leave them and go to another school the following year? It bothered me that I had changed schools so often. Again, my input was not considered in decisions like these, so I never understood why, nor had my feelings validated. Further fuel to the resentment.

It was university that brought a sense of normalcy for once. I finally had the opportunity to stay at a particular school for a while longer than a year or two since my move. My university experiences birthed so many things in and for me – one of them was the stable sense of belonging for the first time in a long time. I had my mini tribe and I loved it.

The journey of an immigrant is such a unique one – moving to a foreign country and finding your feet is no small feat. It is one laced with lots of challenges, disappointments, hope, opportunity, loss, adaptation, change, resilience, uncommon drive, trauma, success, failures, hustle, investment, ingratitude & gratitude; to mention a few.

Although my *japa* experience came with its own unique set of challenges and triumphs, I know that it could have been worse. Hearing the experiences of others in similar yet different shoes to yours, really does put things into perspective.

Of course, it hasn't been all doom and gloom. The truth is, it has afforded me so many opportunities for "the greater good" as mama and papa envisaged, and I am truly so grateful for the sacrifices that Aunty Adaego made for it to happen. However, two things can be true at the same time. The other truth is that it has come at a cost for me too. From time to time, I wonder whether the not-so-great (possibly traumatic) experiences of japa and its impact especially on me were *really* worth it for the opportunities?

Was japa really a good idea?...

3.

Identity

Who are you?

From a very young age, the need to be observant, domestic, respectful, and resourceful was hammered in my consciousness; as an Ada*, the first and only daughter of my family; I had to be these things. The rationale came from the cultural perspective that I was a young girl who would grow into a woman and be married someday. Therefore, my ability to make and keep a home needed to be imbibed from a young age. Although I grew up a Nigerian and Igbo, this reality, I'm sure, is not only particular to my kind.

Validation from others became my nourishment. I quickly learnt how to comply – it was always "yes." I did not know how to say no.

Without realising, this need to do and perform in order to be, translated into everything I did and became the core of my identity. I would do my best to be on top at the schools I attended back home. We were ranked from first to last on our termly report cards and I worked hard to attain and retain a top position, so much so I was known for that.

At work, the same principle applied even in my relationships. In everything really, I always strived to be the best.

The principle in and of itself is not a bad thing – diligence is good, doing is good. However, making that the core of who I was, was not sustainable.

I remember the first time this thought-process and habit of mine was challenged. I was 20 then.

It was a beautiful Sunday morning. The weather was *actually* warm and sunny (if you live in the UK, you would understand why '*actually*' is such a key word!)

I made my way to church.

It was the *Youth Service Sunday* at my church. Youth Service Sunday was typically every month when all the activities were led by the youth. It was a great opportunity for all young individuals to serve and grow in their various giftings.

Jared had the task of teaching and walked up to the pulpit to begin. Jared was someone I looked up to. I admired how transparent he was in talking about his faith walk. He was young and relatable. Although we were not particularly close, we had exchanged conversations a few times and from then, he struck me as someone who was full of wisdom, creativity and a great student of the Bible. Everyone at church could attest to this.

I was very expectant for his teaching and brought out my phone, opened my notes app and waited patiently for him to proceed.

He prayed, then began.

*"The title of the sermon today is, "**Let your light shine: the spotlight is on you!**"* he said.

My fingers typed so quickly as though they had a brain and were perhaps anxious never to miss a thing. He went on to highlight some verses from the Bible as context for his teaching – Isaiah 60: 1-3, Isaiah 43:1 and 1 Peter 2:9.

But before he proceeded with his teaching, he asked the congregation a question: *"**Who are you?**"* – a simple, yet, complex question…

I paused – his voice and everything else slowly drowning in the thoughts of my mind. I could feel my mind doing some algorithms. For some reason, this question caught me by surprise.

After some thought, I murmured to myself: "Well, my name is Adaọra. I'm a student. I work part- time…"

As though the 'play button' to my attention had been turned on simultaneously, just as my mind was trying to fathom and come up with all these ideas of who I thought I was, I heard him say… *"**You are not defined by what you do. What you do should be a by-product of who you***

are; so, I ask you again, who are you?"

That hit me! Echoed by the silence from the congregation following this revelation, I was certain that it caught the majority of us by surprise too.

It hit me because I defined myself primarily by what I did. I mean, how else was I supposed to?

I remember leaving church reflecting on that question.

Who am I… really? Asides what I did or what I have been told to do? What brings me joy and why? What do I like or don't like and why? What are my habits and why? – such uncomfortable, yet necessary questions; especially the why's.

I guess I could say that teaching triggered my journey to uncovering my identity – a journey I knew to embark on after that day. Otherwise, I feared up until that point, I may have been going through life on autopilot, embodying or accepting an identity that was never mine, but one that had been projected from society, family, friends; even my experiences.

Identity refers to a sense of self and a sense of worth:

A sense of self – "the durable core of who you are regardless of the many hats you may wear."

A sense of worth – "what makes you feel significant and confident of your value"

I tend to make what I did, the quality and validation that came from that, the measure of my worth. Although, that may be valid to an extent, allowing it to be the core of my identity was fickle.

The months following that Sunday was accompanied by a quest to truly understand what identity looked like for me, especially as someone who is consistently growing in her faith with God. I stumbled across a teaching on the topic of identity by the late Timothy Keller; an American Pastor, Theologian and Apologist.

In his teaching, he highlighted that: *"any identity that is achieved rather than received is excluding."*

In other words, the worthiness of such identity is derived by comparing against the next person. For example, I may feel worthy because I am smart, pretty or rich. Not just that, but because I am smarter, prettier or richer than the next person which becomes performance based. It is fickle because what happens if someone else is smarter, prettier or richer than me? What happens if I am not smart enough or pretty enough according to a certain standard?

There will always be someone more *fill in the blank* than me, so if that is the measure of worthiness, it is excluding to me. That inevitably means that I am not as worthy...

"It is unsustainable," he emphasised.

I sat with that for a moment.

He further went on to explain that in our culture, there are various narratives on how to discover our identity which are not sustainable; one of them being to look inward and decide who we are. He maintained that although there is a role for introspection, self-awareness and assertion, there are a few reasons why this approach might not be accurate as the *sole* basis to define who we are:

- *It can be incoherent – it does not always match up to who we truly are. The way we perceive ourselves is influenced by our experiences, society, opinions of others; our deepest feelings can contradict each other.*
- *It is unstable – our inward feelings and desires are constantly changing.*
- *It is illusory – our feelings are discordant, and you have to choose. There is a grid influenced by culture.*
- *It is burdensome – because it relies solely on you. "When you make what you do and the quality of what you do your identity, they stop being good things." In other words, there's pressure to always outdo what you have previously done. Whilst, this pressure can be a great way to challenge oneself, what happens on the occasions you cannot? How do you see yourself?*

- *It is excluding – i.e., it is performance based and relies on how worthy you are compared to the next person?*

I understood that perfectly. If I was to define myself, it would have been by what I did, my experiences or what society said I should become.

"So, how do I define myself?" I wondered.

His teaching further expanded on this:

"We are relational beings that crave for validation or recognition. For validation to be validation, it should come outside of you – the love, approval, and esteem of someone you'd esteem, if you don't have any self-esteem. For sustainability, this person cannot be fickle or let you down.

The only person inherently capable by nature for this is God.

The Lord and Creator of the whole universe; loving us is the most powerful basis for a stable identity possible.

He is the Creator and only One worthy of naming and validating us because He made us. His love for us is not based on performance and therefore, is not excluding whatsoever. His love is a gift displayed by the death of Jesus on the Cross to restore us back to our identity. We are created, known, loved, validated and named by God. This should be the core of our sense of worth; every other thing is secondary. This is such a beautiful reality because it bestows upon one the worth, significance and value that transcends performance, achievements and situations. Whether I am rich or poor or situations change, I am eternally valued and loved by God and that is enough," he concluded.

I laid on my bed as my cheeks caught the solemn drops of my tears like a dam. I could not believe what I just heard. **breathe in, breathe out**…it felt like a huge burden had been lifted off my shoulders! My mind wrestled with the reality and magnitude of this kind of love.

It felt like for the first time, I was offered a love that I did not have to earn or strive for.

That teaching marked me.

Since that day, I have been on the journey of learning and unlearning. Unlearning the many ways, I have made the core of my identity what it should have never been and learning how to truly become from a place of unshakeable security.

Although I was born into a Christian household, my personal journey of faith really started in my 20s.

On this journey of uncovering my identity, I couldn't help but begin to see how I had fallen again into this trap of making what I did; my performance, the basis of my identity, *even* within my faith – maybe if I go to church every Sunday, then I am worthy enough. Maybe if I pray hard enough, then I am worthy.

I began to see many ways I had slipped into self-righteousness; constantly trying to outdo the next Christian to feel better than. Seeing spiritual disciplines as the qualifiers of my faith instead of faith itself. Doing things to be seen and applauded relative to a place of rest. Forgetting that faith is a gift received through God alone.

God's love is a gift – it takes faith in Jesus Christ to receive it. Everything else I need and should do for God should be born from a place of love received and not to receive love. But I thought I could earn it. My need to please others had translated in my spiritual walk.

I wrestled with receiving such pure love without feeling like I had to earn it.

Through prayer and a constant reminder of God's love and grace through scripture, I began to embrace such love that has been given and started learning to rest in it.

I became grateful for an identity that is grounded in truth and is unshakeable. I am created and loved by God, so I am enough.

Before I am anything else or the many hats I may wear; before whom and where I was born and the things that have happened and shaped me in some ways…first and foremost, is that I am loved by God, and fearfully and wonderfully made by Him. This is not something I earn; it has already been given. It is who I am once I identify with and receive this faith through Jesus Christ. What a beautiful reality to have an identity at the core that is dependent on the One who is unchanging. Everything else is extra.

This reality has been healing to me and has sieved through narratives I had embodied that are not in alignment with who I truly am.

Narratives that echoed my need *to do* in order *to be* valued and loved, narratives that communicate any unworthiness, negative stories I constantly told myself as a result of some of my experiences that had to be unlearnt.

A hard, but necessary action.

4.

"What would you like to be when you grow up?"

I wanted to be so many things – a paediatrician, a journalist, an author, a chef with her own cooking show, a pharmacist, a philanthropist – an ever-changing list of things.

I miss dreaming as a child. There were no barriers. The older I got, *reality* hit. Indeed, *reality* has a great way of ushering some level of pessimism if you let it.

On Tuesday 23rd March 2021, a Microsoft Teams message popped up on my work laptop. It was from Tasha and it read:

"Hey Adaora, Happy 1-year anniversary . Not sure about you but it's gone very quickly... Hope you are all okay?"

I paused; my brain frantically trying to translate the meaning of this message.

Then, it dawned on me!

It had been one year since I got my very first "big girl" job (graduate role).

"Oh, my goodness! I can't believe it has been one year already! Wow! Thank you so much T, I'm all okay thank you. Happy one-year anniversary to you too! How are you? Hope you are okay?" I responded.

She was right; the year had gone by very quickly. Two promotions in, multiple meltdowns, lots of anxious moments and embracing change including starting a new role remotely due to a global pandemic; we had both made it to one year of full-time work. Tasha and I both started our jobs in the same organisation on the same day, although we worked in different teams and what a journey it had been.

Transitioning post-university into full-time work had been daunting. To start with, I did not get this job immediately after graduating. It was only after what seemed like a plethora of rejections that I eventually secured it. The rejections did a number on my psyche; I did not fathom that it was a part of the application process, so it was a shock to my system.

University was somewhat a safety blanket for me. Although I still had responsibilities at university like balancing studies with working part-time and gaining various other work experiences, paying my rent and other bills etc, which was not easy; adulting had taken a whole new level since transitioning to full-time work as a graduate.

From figuring out what awaited me after university, to navigating the job-hunting process which was long and tedious – why didn't anyone warn me? Tailoring my CV and writing new cover letters to match various job descriptions each time was not on my bingo card, but it had to be done.

Eventually, about a year later, I secured a role which is the one Tasha celebrated during the 1-year anniversary.

Anything to do with adulting so far, seems to be such a journey and navigating the world of work was no exception to the rule. The working world is an ecosystem on its own with set principles and guidance that underpin it. Adapting my personality and perspective whilst navigating this world has been a skill I've had to quickly learn and develop. Intersectionality was not a word in my vocabulary prior to my professional working experience, but now, it is not just a word but a concept I completely acknowledge and recognise.

Intersectionality:

"A recognition that each part of a person's multifaceted identity – race, ethnicity, gender and other traits has a dramatic influence on the way they interact with employers and other institutions. While the various components of a person's identity lend unique perspectives on work and life, they can also lead to distinct career obstacles and discrimination."

Understanding this concept was very key in giving me language to some of my experiences in the first year of my work.

"I can't seem to read you", were words Karen, my first manager said to me in one of our 1-2-1 check-ins. She alluded to the fact that she could read everyone else in our team because they were loud and outspoken. I, on the other hand, "*was quiet and reserved*" and she had an issue with it.

When I probed whether she felt this was having an impact on the work I was doing, she acknowledged that it wasn't, but it was something she felt the need to call out.

I didn't understand what the problem with being quiet and reserved was all about. Afterall, I was there to get my work done and we don't all have to be loud and outspoken. We are all different!

I would eventually come to find out that Karen's issue was that I didn't participate in 'office gossip…' When things were said in meetings about other colleagues and I was present, I usually don't involve myself in those types of discussions. I was not used to such culture and did not engage with it because it did not align with my values as an individual.

I guess it made her and perhaps some others, uncomfortable. I contributed to work-related discussions, did my presentations, had successfully line managed two staff members at the time, so if there was an issue regarding my social competence, those examples should have challenged that.

Understanding, appreciating, and cultivating a workplace where intersectionality thrives takes work and most times, people would rather not do that.

Having said that, in principle, I would come to find out that Karen was partly right: being loud (about achievements) in the workplace was very key for progression.

As a fresh (naïve) graduate keen to make an impression, I wasted no time in making attempts 'to hit the ground running' in my first role – zeal is great, but zeal without boundaries is detrimental to self. Without realising, I began to attach my worth to work, and began finding work overwhelming as a result.

In hindsight, I was burnt out. It felt like I always had so much to do and was drowning under it all. I was at a place where I literally had zero motivation to do my job. I was over it! The frustrating part of my lack of motivation at the time was the actual work not stopping whether I felt like it or not. I was inundated with an ever-growing to-do list and what seemed like a plethora of work requests that needed my attention.

Though I masked it well, I then struggled to line manage the colleagues under my supervisory as a result – you really cannot pour from an empty cup.

As a ripple effect, I quickly began to feel like an imposter and internalised what I was going through when in fact, I should have recognised I needed a break from work.

"Soul-destroying" was how Aisha described work to me once. She worked in consulting at the time but was on placement at my work temporarily. I remember laughing apologetically at this response because I hadn't heard anyone describe work using those words. In the same breadth, I could also empathise.

There is a narrative that suggests the best thing to do when it comes to work and building a career is for one to do what is enjoyable 'and never work a day' in their life. Whilst I can appreciate the sentiment behind this narrative, it does not negate the fact that even with the things I am passionate about, it takes work to pursue and execute them. In other words, there is no escaping "work."

Learning to separate my worth from my work has been helpful in allowing me to receive criticism well. I can filter through feedback without internalising them as a direct reflection on who I am. It is not always an easy thing to do, but it's well worth it.

Thoughts on building a career

Two years into working a 9-5 and I still was not sure what I ***really*** wanted to do. In fact, I remember questioning if the concept of work was for me.

But of course, the reality of my bills and circumstances awoke me from that daydream immediately. The issue was, being age 25 felt like I should already *know* what my long-term plan career-wise, was.

"You're still young! You don't have to figure it all out right now. Now is the time to explore, so start." Angela said on an MS Teams call. I had scheduled a 1-2-1 with her to brainstorm and process my concerns on trying to figure out a career path and that was her initial advice.

Angela was one of my seniors at work in her 40s. She was someone I looked up to; an expert in her own right doing so well for herself. She had lots of work experiences under her belt and was settled on a career path as a Black British African woman.

What was supposed to be a 30-minute quick chat segway-ed into an hour and half meeting. The good news was that I came out feeling inspired and ready to persevere on the journey ahead, being challenged and encouraged. Angela highlighted many other key things, some of which she already challenged me on during my short career span at the time:

Advocating for myself:

Advocating for myself and managing perception at work was something I had to learn. I was privy to build a solid rapport with Angela. On previous occasions, she shared her journey to where she was (which I considered at 'the top.') It was immediately clear on hearing her story that she had journeyed through so much to get to where she was.

It didn't happen overnight, and her journey wasn't void of challenges either – there was a lot of hardwork, navigating self-doubt, people doubting her worth, imposter syndrome; the list goes on. Living in an unfair world meant the workplace, unfortunately, isn't exempt. Thus, she shared stories of some of the unfairness she encountered by being a Black British African woman in the workplace.

She made it one of her missions to ensure I was equipped to advocate for myself.

"No one is going to give you permission to speak," was one of her many gems that stuck with me. She alluded to the fact that there is a place for assertiveness in the workplace, and it was solely up to me to assert myself. As someone who is introverted, conflict-averse or shall I say, *previously* conflict-averse, assertiveness was a challenge. It felt like confrontation, and I tended to 'let things slide.'

Similarly, it was unlike me to 'shout about' the things I did for work. I assumed it was obvious, so I'd rather get the job done and keep it moving. I had to learn that communicating what I was doing was paramount and had to be *seen* working by *verbally championing the tasks I completed* no matter how obvious I thought it may be.

This experience of mine was validated by an excerpt from probably one of the most hilarious but surprisingly accurate books I've ever read: [9]

"Doing a great piece of work or coming up with a great idea is useless unless it is done within eye or earshot of someone who can, and probably will do something to propel you forward in return. So, a smart professional only does things that really matter in front of people who matter."

Although this excerpt might sound dramatic, there's a lot of truth in it. And though I'd say, "*do a diligent work no matter who is looking*", I honestly do get the author's logic.

Angela was right about advocating for myself though.

"The workplace can be like a jungle, so it is important to stand your ground, bet on yourself and be loud about it. Set clear boundaries; be assertive. It will help manage people's perceptions too." Her words helped relieve these shoulders of mine which were laced with naivety and overwhelm.

Our communities contribute to the people we are today. Angela was one of them for me. She was God-sent and I am forever grateful for her wisdom.

I still don't have all the answers, nor the entire picture when it comes to my career and navigating it. Heck, I still do not have a clear picture on where I am exactly headed. But what I do know is that my approach to work is not what it used to be because of growth. It's not what it used to be because of people like Angela on my path.

Thankfully, my faith also continuously challenges and grounds the way I see and engage with work. Rather than seeing it as one laborious cycle, which it can be, I see it as something *I get to do* as stewardship; something that has been gifted to me by God to manage and execute on His behalf. This mindset has been beneficial, especially in moments of apathy and continues to help inspire excellence.

Do I have it all figured out now? Absolutely **not!** Have I grown over the course of the years? **Yes!**

Adulting has taught me to celebrate my wins and lately, I have chosen to see growth as a win too.

5.

Redefining Success for Me

When it comes to success, the goalpost is forever shifting. If it is not getting a first-class degree, it is building a five-figure business. If it is not the five figures, it is making the Forbes under 30 list. You name it!

Social media does not make it any easier too. Being exposed to people's success from time to time can make it harder to acknowledge that behind every success, must have been some failures too. Or, that everyone has unique circumstances. Thus, I would be doing myself a disservice to blatantly aspire for the same on face-value without considering *and* establishing what I want success to look like for me.

Whilst all of the five-figure business, first class degrees and the likes are fantastic feats, I have come to the resolve that it will be unrealistic to personally have them as the umbrella benchmark as success for myself.

I have thought about whether my new-found resolve is a way of pacifying myself, but I don't think that is completely the case. I am becoming more comfortable with the idea that success most times, looks a lot more mundane for me. This does not negate the need for ambition of course. It's great to have ambition; however, I do not need to consciously on subconsciously take on added goals or pressures that were never mine in the first place.

Success for me lately has taken on a more daily approach and what some people would describe as 'small wins' – so if I make it to the gym like I said I would? Success. If I commit to making that phone call I have been putting off? Success. If I make it through that job interview (because interviews give me some anxiety?) Success. If I consistently build on my healthy habits? Success. If I only barely make it through the day? Success!

In other words, a success that acknowledges my humanity and affords me the grace to be and become, is success to me. Life is already tough please.

The shift in perspective has been quite ironic for me because I used to strongly desire to be in the Forbes under 30 list. I wasn't quite sure what for, but it was a dream at some point. A major contributor to that desire is the fact that it seems quite validating and frankly, *'badass.'* It still is. Who wouldn't want to be recognised on such a scale for 'badass-ness' in their field?! Perhaps it is my innate Nigerian child's need to make her parents proud…

I know mama and papa would be exceptionally proud if this dream of mine actually came to pass. In fact, I'm sure of it. I remember the time I was featured on the radio as one of the best students from my last school before japa*. The entire community did not hear the end of it for a while from papa's lips. Or was it when I eventually graduated from university with a first-class degree?! Let's just say that papa made sure to always introduce me with that line. *"This is my first-class graduate, daughter, Adaora!"*

So of course, that desire to please them and make them proud also manifests in my pursuit of success.

Notwithstanding, I am constantly challenging my motivation behind the 'kind of success' I want to pursue and why. Pursuing things just because of the idea of validation is not sustainable. Am I demonising pursuing things for the sake of validation? No, but it is not sustainable if that is the core or main reason. I definitely do not want to fall into the previous trap of attaching my identity to something so fickle.

Do I still want to be a part of the Forbes list lowkey? Absolutely. The difference now is that it is not a hill I am willing to die on. If it happens, amazing! If not, my worthiness and how successful I deem myself to be, is not hinged on this – it is easier said than done though as with most of these things.

Having community that celebrates even what I might consider 'small wins' has been so pivotal in helping to reshape the way I view success.

Mama is my biggest cheerleader! She celebrates my every win no matter how insignificant I think they might be.

When I had bought my small second hand, 1.2L car, mama gloated over the phone like I had just won the lottery or discovered the cure to cancer.

"Agu nwanyi!*", mama exclaimed with so much excitement.

Agu nwanyi: A lioness; a woman who does everything including those that are exclusive reserves of men. A woman that displays prowess in what she does. A tigress. A strong woman, as strong as a lion or Tigress."

This was her way of praising my doggedness. Her happiness was infectious, and it eventually rubbed off on me.

Prior to her reaction and as crazy as it sounds, I didn't think it was a big deal. It wasn't a brand-new car, neither was it a Mercedes so 'it wasn't that deep'. People buy better cars and were doing better things than I had just done – that was how I perceived the win at the time.

Imagine. How could I let comparison taint my perception like that?!

Mama's celebration jolted the true reality of what I had done and made me realise that this achievement was in fact, ***that deep.*** Being able to be diligent enough to save up and eventually buy a car was a big deal. I appreciated her hailing and praising me for this feat so much. It put things into perspective and made me content and proud of this win.

What does success look like for me? What is driving the type of success I'm seeking and why have I classed whatever it is as success? Why is 'success' important to me? – just like mama's reaction was a reminder, these are some questions which constantly keep me grounded in my pursuit.

PART II

Unlearning is hard.

6.

Boundaries

"You can't build a boundary with someone else if you don't build one with yourself," Dr. Kari said. Her words wrapped in a missile of conviction. Her eyes directly staring back at mine as though if it could speak; it was to communicate the need for me to truly understand and apply this.

It had been a few weeks since I started therapy. At this point, I wasn't exactly sure if I had made the right decision by going. Dr. Kari wasn't the first therapist I was assigned to. I had to change my initial therapist as I felt he rushed me – with his time, he was always busy and would stress the need to 'hurry and book a slot with him before it is gone' from the jump!

That wasn't very helpful as it was my first-time trialling therapy, and it took a lot to decide to commit to it. The last thing I wanted was for anyone to make me feel like a commodity. Therapy is such a vulnerable process and the least I expected was for some patience and accommodation for my schedule too.

So, I decided to switch therapists. I found Dr. Kari on my second attempt. She was welcoming and accommodating.

By the end of this session, I was coming to yet another realisation that I had no boundaries.

Of course, I didn't. I didn't even know what they really were in the first place…

Although I had heard of the word due to the many recent discourses about boundaries, I didn't know what it meant and what it looked like, practically.

Through my sessions with her, I learnt that boundaries are essentially a way of telling people how to treat me; setting expectations on how I would like to be treated.

"Boundaries are necessary for your relationships especially in order to have healthy relationships where you feel safe and respected. They can be implicit or explicit:

***Implicit** will look like having a sign on the door outside your room to communicate that you will be having a meeting and need no distractions whilst you are working from home.*

***Explicit** will look like telling whoever is at home, not to interrupt whilst you work"* she said.

From her example, I liked the sound of implicit boundaries. Having a sign that communicated the message so people 'got the memo' was more appealing to me. I guess that was rooted in my avoidant nature when it came to anything that seemed like confrontation.

When I went on to openly reflect on the fact that I didn't think I had *any* boundaries following our conversations in that session, she chimed in:

"That may not be entirely true. You can have boundaries but they might be poor. It sounds like you have what we call porous boundaries – you know how you would like to be treated, but struggle to assert boundaries. Do you find that you tend to overextend yourself or say yes when you really want to say no?", she challenged.

"Yes! Sounds pretty accurate," I murmured. The murmuring was synonymous to my thinking of how this was yet another episode of Dr. Kari reading me.

That session and the following sessions after opened my eyes.

As homework over these sessions, she gave me resources to aid in my reflection and understanding. These resources included recommended books to read.

One of which explored some of the different types of boundaries. My homework was to read and write a summary of my understanding of these different boundary types to personalise some examples for myself:

Some types of boundaries include:

***Physical boundaries** – this refers to preferences or expectations around physical space or touch. e.g. would I rather shake someone's hand than hug them? Do I hate it when people are all up in my physical space? Setting physical boundaries is expressing preferences around these.*

***Emotional boundaries** – this refers to preferences or expectations on how I expect others to support me when I am vulnerable or share my feelings. For me, expressing my emotions is never easy, so I pay attention to how people respond when I eventually find the courage to. Having emotional boundaries means I choose my confidants carefully or not sharing too much information inappropriately.*

***Material boundaries** – this has to do with my possessions and how I decide to share my things, or how I expect others to treat my possessions. For example, if I have loaned an item of mine, I expect it to be in the same condition as it was when it was lent, not worse!*

***Sexual boundaries** – self-explanatory. Consent is key. "Touching, making sexual comments or engaging in sexual acts without expressed consent is a violation of sexual boundaries."*

It was interesting to observe in my study and reflection on boundaries that there can be what is called **rigid** boundaries too. This was the other extreme where people do in fact have boundaries, but these are so rigid that it leaves no leeway for manoeuvring, grace, and community. People with rigid boundaries tend to cut people off quickly, ghost or are unable to be open and vulnerable. That really stood out to me because there can be the subtle temptation of equating having boundaries, as having *rigid* boundaries when the two are not necessarily the same.

"I cannot lie, learning how to set boundaries for myself and communicating them has not been easy for me. I really struggle with telling people exactly what I desire clearly and firmly. I would rather be passive and let things slide. I eventually get upset at people's reaction even though I didn't clearly state my expectations." I sighed.

Dr. Kari met my frustration with empathy.

"Why do you think that is?" she gently probed further.

I released yet another sigh before responding.

"I don't know. I mean, the latter is mostly rooted in the fact that I often expect people to 'know better.' The main reason would be that I would rather avoid any type of confrontation all together."

Dr. Kari and I would go on a journey of uncovering the root to my thoughts and responses when it came to boundaries.

There were traces to childhood and experiences ushered by *japa.* Being in an environment that wasn't safe enough did not help to facilitate my ability to express how I was feeling.

I expressed how for as long as I could remember; there was this internal pressure to always comply and not challenge things or anyone (especially in authority).

We excavated previous responses that implicitly introduced and reinforced this notion of mine. The same notion that echoed it was disrespectful to express my thoughts, disagree with or challenge things – for example:

"You must respect your elders!"

"Why are you asking me questions? Am I your mate?"

"Z!" – (a sarcastic and condescending response when asked why)

My opinions had previously been met with some level of backlash enough to discourage any future expressions of mine. As a result, I became unable to set healthy boundaries.

We also uncovered a fear of being shouted at. Even as an adult, I had subtle fear that I was going to be shouted at if I spoke my mind. To avoid it, I became mute and passive, suppressing how I truly felt and not communicating, which was reflective in my relationships.

I once read that '*some children are trained to be seen, not heard and are taught that asking for what they want or having healthy boundaries is disrespectful. Thus, as adults, they find it difficult to shake this way of thinking off*' – and I couldn't agree more because it echoed my reality.

My difficulty in setting and communicating boundaries was rooted in fear – how would they (whoever I was setting a boundary with) react? What if things become awkward? What if their attitude changes towards me?

It was also rooted in guilt. I felt so bad for setting them like I had no permission to. The guilt was overwhelming that it deterred me from wanting to assert boundaries.

Little did I know that it was actually a part of the process of boundary-setting. Particularly, for someone like me who wasn't used to *not* complying as much. It was inevitable and I had to come to terms with it.

I am learning that feelings of guilt shouldn't hinder me from setting boundaries anyway. As one of the resources Dr. Kari recommended pointed out, *'There is no such thing as guilt-free boundaries'* [10]

No matter how challenging setting boundaries were for me, I had to persevere past the discomfort that came with it. Being passive-aggressive or any other approach other than assertive with boundaries led to resentment, burnout, people-pleasing, anxiety, depression, anger, frustration, gossip and complaints. A little confrontation and backlash seemed like the appropriate price to pay for my sanity and for the preservation of my relationships.

One major conviction I had about my initial inability of setting boundaries was the inauthenticity at the core of it. A fundamental aspect of boundary-setting is integrity. How am I being true to myself and others if I do not clearly and directly communicate my feelings or expectations? How do relationships deepen and evolve if things are let to slide or swept under the carpet?

"Communicating our boundaries isn't easy, but without it, we set ourselves up for long-term suffering. We simply can't have a healthy relationship with another person without communicating what is acceptable and unacceptable to us. If we are not proactive about this in our relationships, we can be sure the other person will set their boundaries. That forces us to operate by their rules and their rules only."
– An excerpt: Set Boundaries; find peace a guide to reclaiming yourself by Nedra Glover Tawwab.

The journey of learning about boundaries and applying it does not only challenge me to be a better individual relationally, but more than that; I have found it is challenging and is also preparing me to become a better parent in the near future. I am beginning to grasp how delicate the formative years are and how it might be challenging for a parent. Thus, I'm constantly being challenged on this journey to unlearn unhealthy patterns of behaviours, so I can be a better model for my children.

Each time I think about it, I am reminded of how big of a responsibility it is to raise a human being to become whole, healthy and well-rounded. It's a lot! This realisation has somewhat allowed me to give grace to the people that raised me for the times they did not get it right, whilst healing from their wrongs.

Healing isn't linear. I have learnt to extend grace for the times I didn't know better, the times I should have known better and the times I did not exactly get it right. I've been pacing myself in the application of what I am learning such as communicating my feelings with written words as it feels less intimidating to start with.

Some key reminders since trying to be a boundary babe:

- People react to boundary settings differently – acceptance, silent treatment, defensiveness, testing limits, ignoring, ghosting. Acknowledge, but don't fixate on them. It is not my responsibility to control how people react towards my boundary setting.
- I must follow through with my boundaries. Be intentional about reinforcing them when they are violated. Otherwise, how do I expect people to respect my boundaries when I do not? In other words, let people experience *consequences* for their actions.
- Boundaries evolve as needs change and that's okay. New boundaries ought to be set for different changes or transitory periods in life. Boundaries need to evolve.
- Boundary setting can be uncomfortable and that's okay. It's supposed to be most times.
- I must be willing to accept and respect other people's boundaries too – a tough one I have to master. Somehow, other people setting boundaries with me felt like rejection initially. That is not the case and even if it was, that's okay too. Respect is reciprocal – the same way I would like my boundaries honoured; I must honour that of others too.
- Having boundaries does not negate the act of selflessness from time to time. My boundaries do not have to be rigid.

As a Christian, it is okay to have boundaries which does not negate the role of being selfless. Serving and loving others does not necessarily mean constantly overextending yourself out of fear for not being able to say no. At the core of having boundaries is the freedom to choose. The truth is because we are Christians, that is exactly why we do and *should* have boundaries.

Boundaries are a safeguard for both me and my relationships too. I cannot love others as myself if I do not have any boundaries.

7.

Friendships and Outgrowing Them

After I had left the popular friendship group with all the IT girls due to an unwelcoming experience, I decided to take a break in making friends at my new school post-*japa.* I channelled all the energy I had previously used to try and *fit in* to being a loner for a while and preparing for my exams ahead at the time.

As time progressed, I eventually found a European sister who had approached me whilst I was sat in a corner alone one afternoon. Her green endearing eyes met mine and instantly communicated an 'I see you' moment; I desperately needed it at the time. She was tall with blonde hair and her aura exuded softness as well as confidence. She was unapologetically herself and I loved that about her. We became close and bonded over our shared differences. Though we didn't speak the same language, our hearts did.

It was nice to have a friend whom I shared some level of relatability with, both being immigrants trying to navigate our new world, learning a new culture, and adapting to how different it was to ours. The conversation from our initial encounter was marked by sharing our tales of culture-shock which was so similar! We remained friends until I left that school. This was the friendship that marked the beginning of yet another journey of navigating friendships; this time, in a new environment.

It makes logical sense to expect that one would outgrow certain relationships as they evolved. However, this was a shock as I did not quite consider this. When it eventually happened, I wrestled with the reality of it SO MUCH.

Over the years, some of my friendships have ended. Not necessarily because of drama or issues, but simply because we had evolved, moved on with life and the communication and commitment to each other seized. We grew apart…

I felt extreme guilt for the cessation of some of these friendships when I had done nothing wrong. The guilt was a result of the fact that, I did not like the reality that things had changed between us and could not fathom letting go. I can be quite possessive at times and that did not help in letting go and embracing the new reality. This change in dynamics towards some of my friendships happened a few times before I slowly started coming to terms that this was perhaps a cycle of life? That maybe some people in my life were meant to be present for a season?

This was not an easy reality to comprehend.

On many occasions, I found myself holding onto relationships that had already served their purpose. I knew deep down things were no longer as they used to be and were approaching the end, but I was not willing to let go. Overcompensating due to guilt, I would go all out doing the most to maintain those relationships, literally carrying them on my back. That looked like forcing communication, time and energy into situations that were clearly no longer mutual and making excuses for bad behaviour i.e., lack of respect and consideration. The grand example – forcing a semblance of intimacy that was no longer existent!

Chinenye and I used to be close friends. We both went to the same school in Nigeria since we were children. Interestingly, we both emigrated from Nigeria around the same time – she went to Canada, and I of course moved in with Aunty Adaego to the UK for further education. Prior to this change, we practically spent most of our days together.

Notwithstanding, we were both happy to experience similar changes at the time. We could not wait for our constant calls which doubled as a debrief session for the newness we were experiencing. In the first two years of our move, we maintained constant communication. She was a safe space as I navigated my newfound home, and was one of the reasons aside God, that helped with my sanity.

However, as time went on, the dynamics of our friendship began to change. Our conversations were no longer as consistent. At first, I thought it was a temporary hiccup in our relationship. I mean, we were both in new environments, trying to adapt and find our feet amid other things that life was throwing at us.

However, with each passing day of what seemed like forced conversations, the change in dynamics was reaffirmed. It became clear that she was changing as a person and our core values no longer aligned.

In denial of this truth, I still held on. Another three additional years into this discovery, I would still reach out from time to time when it was evidently clear that I was now the only one doing the communicating. It was clear that the commitment of the friendship was now one-sided, but this was my attempt to maintain the relationship and preserve how it used to be.

Again, the guilt of letting go hovered over my head for so long. What about all those years of investment? The good times we had and shared? How we both promised to be there for each other no matter what? How was I meant to carry on journeying life without someone who was once my closest friend?

We would go months or an entire year without speaking, but each time it was Chi's birthday, I would feel the need to write a long paragraph like the old times. Of course, nowadays, a person's birthday won't be complete without a massive shoutout on social media, so I would go ahead and do that (even though I knew our bond was no longer strong). I would profess my love for our 'friendship' –very much overcompensating!

There was no need to portray a semblance of intimacy; especially when it was no longer there. It was one of my attempts of convincing myself that this was still a friendship. Eventually, it became exhausting and I had to accept that by overcompensating, I was not being genuine. My motivation to hold unto this relationship was no longer for healthy reasons, but one born out of guilt and fear. That was no longer sustainable. It also bred room for disappointment especially when it was not reciprocated to the capacity I expected. For this reason, I stopped holding on and that was the end...

With Chinenye though, I wish I had explicitly communicated how I genuinely felt about the change between us and how it made me feel. It may have been futile but, could it have been a way to extend grace? Perhaps. I don't really know. At the time, Chinenye's eventual lack of commitment and reciprocity, was a good enough sign for me. For that reason, I did not feel the need to confront and point it out.

My friendship breakup with Chinenye affected me emotionally and I grieved what it once was and what it could have been.

Chinenye was not the only relationship I outgrew. There were a few others for various reasons. All of which challenged my perspective on outgrowing people – it's not such a bad thing.

Outgrowing people, situations and mindsets are all part of adulting. For me, this does not mean that it's not okay to give people the grace they need to evolve. Of course, I believe that. However, I learnt, within reason. Sometimes, giving grace can also look like accepting changes to dynamics and adjusting accordingly. I came to realise that in some instances, I had *casually* accorded the title of 'friend' too quickly and simply needed to adjust my expectations, instead of cutting people off entirely.

The word 'outgrowing' has a negative connotation as subconsciously, it can suggest something bad happening to trigger ones' change of mind, but mine and Chinenye's case proved otherwise. Growth and change are constant and necessary; it doesn't always need a negative catalyst.

Of course, there could be other negative triggers to a friendship breakup including betrayal, dishonesty, abuse, etc, but in our case, it was simply the fact that life happens, and people change. I had to also accept that it does not negate the good of the friendship too.

Would I have loved a friendship group with most of my friends from childhood who evolved together with me? Absolutely! Unfortunately, that was not my reality and there is nothing wrong with it.

I currently have a few mixes of friends I've known for different lengths of time. Some of my friends I have known since university days over six years+. Others, over three years, and some under a year. I'm learning that asides the length of time, it is the depth and quality of the friendship that is important.

<u>A note on friendships that are seasonal</u>

Since grieving some of my friendships that were seasonal, the thought of 'seasonal friendships' scared me. In fact, the thought of making friends as an adult in general scared me. I became more guarded when making friends. Making friends in my 20s has been a journey, but this mindset did not make it easier.

Due to the fear of grieving yet another end to a friendship, I constantly wondered if there was a point of making new friends and shyed away from the idea on many occasions. In some of my friendships, I would take any sign of healthy conflict as another friendship on the brink of a breakup. I was constantly anxious which was exhausting. I had enough and decided this was not a sustainable way to live life. I had to make peace with the fact that though some friendships might be seasonal, it shouldn't be a deterrent to new connections.

The older I got, the more I realised that I **need** community. I need people. I need friends. Whether they are there for a season or a lifetime, I owe it to myself to embrace it; to love without bars and no regrets if it ends. This does not negate the fact that it stings when dynamics change or the expectations of the future I once had for my friendships may not actualise. I owe it to myself not to let past hurt hinder the present and future experiences of friendships no matter how short lived.

Seasonal friendships are still friendships. Instead of resenting them, I am choosing to savour the memories.

8.

A Friend like Zara

"I used to envy people with a large friendship group that was solid. I wanted what they had. I mean, how did they manage to keep all these friends through their years of evolution thus far?"

Zara could sense the seriousness in my voice…

She chuckled and followed with a reply: *"Maybe they are just lucky, sis!"*

The calming sounds of the waves at Margate beach crashed against the shore where we were sat as though it agreed with her sentiment. It was a fine summer afternoon, and we decided to go on a spontaneous trip to the beach. The topic of discussion that day was a range of things including the challenges of friendships as adults and how difficult it can be to make new friends or maintain them as we got older.

Zara and I became friends at the latter part of my life shortly after university. We met at a youth fellowship. She was a year younger than me and at the time, we had been friends for just over a year. Prior to the day we had this conversation, we hadn't seen each other in five months, so this was a long overdue catchup in person. A catchup we had been planning for almost just as long.

The conversation was so fitting to our reality of friendship as we had been reflecting on the intentionality required to maintain our union whilst navigating many other things going on in our lives. Zara had moved to a new city, started a new job and was working on her passion projects at the time while I, on the other hand, was settling into a new role and trying to figure that out as well.

We caught up. We laughed. We shared our hearts with each other including how best we could show up and support each other, amid the busyness of our lives and schedules as we were both in transitory phases. I appreciated this conversation because it was so necessary for me. If there was one thing I learned the hard way with my various friendship dynamics, it was that unspoken assumptions or expectations are usually a recipe for disaster and disappointment. I really wasn't the best at expressing my needs to people, so having friends like Zara who challenged me in this way was necessary.

"I miss the days when convenience was not such a luxury," Zara lamented. A resolve I could relate to. She explained how friendships were easier when we were much younger at school. There was always the opportunity to see your friends every day and spend time with them; most of them even lived in the same neighbourhood! It was very much convenient.

However, the older we got, this was stripped away by the very hands of adulting. With a million and one things to do, to process and navigate, all of a sudden, time became an expensive commodity with intentionality being the price. We had to now be intentional about checking in on each other and making space for each other. In addition to that, facilitating a safe space for each other and being accountable.

Facilitating growth and making sure friendships are not superficial but one with depth, championed by honesty, transparency, communication, vulnerability, authenticity, and trust are all essential components of a thriving friendship. "The older I get, the more I cherish my friends with depth. Friends I can be myself with," she paused.

Taking another deep breath, she continued: "You know…friends I won't be afraid to be vulnerable with who challenge me to grow or evolve for the better and tell the truth in love and gentleness. Friends who encourage and speak life over me, friends with wise Godly counsel, supportive friends who understand me and are patient, who emulate and show grace, friends who inspire and help me grow in various areas in my life, friends who genuinely and actively love me, friends I enjoy…"

As she spoke, my mind couldn't help but wonder if I was truly such a friend to her but also how much ***work*** that takes.

"That's work!" I blurted out. Simultaneously, we shook our heads in agreement.

That was the truth – such type of friendship takes grace and work to be built. Investing time in truly getting to know, understand and supporting my friends is a hefty task. Getting to know someone can take years of intent or experiencing life with them and isn't always easy, alongside trying to navigate the hustle and bustle of life. However, it is very much possible and needed.

What is Grace? – Making allowance for a friend's fault.

It may not be easy but it is required in friendships. Giving grace is not an excuse for bad behaviour. However, in navigating my adult friendships, I have come to a heightened understanding that my friends are not perfect and neither am I. There is a level of selflessness and commitment required in friendships.

As Zara and I tarried in our conversation on friendships and how we can become better towards each other, we decided to write down some of our realisations in navigating friendships as adults. We called this ***the friendship reflections checklist.***

My friendship reflections checklist read:

- *I might not see my friends or talk to them every day. Of course, I'd still make plans to see them as often as I can, but if that's not possible, that's okay.*
- *My friends navigate life and all its issues in different ways.*
- *My friends might need to process things first before they confide in me.*
- *My friends have boundaries I must respect.*
- *They might not always get some things right.*
- *I do not have ownership over my friends.*
- *My friends can have other friend's asides me (LOL – this is a silly but tough one because I can be quite possessive).*
- *Friendships grow and evolve and that's life. Take stock and re-evaluate. It's okay to outgrow some friendships if need be.*

- *My friends are* ***not*** mind *readers. Phew! I wish they were! That's one thing I love about my relationship with Jesus; He is omniscient and I appreciate it so much. The best friend ever. Unfortunately, my real-life friends obviously aren't and can't always guess my needs, so I need to speak up – still a work in progress...*
- *I have to be open and vulnerable with my friends to build friendships with depth.*
- *I need the grace to steward my friendships so I must talk to God about them.*
- *Communication, honesty, intentionality, mutual respect and forgiveness are an integral part of adult friendships.*

Zara's friendship reflections checklist read:

- *Friendship has offered me comfort; a sense of belonging, love, care and a place of safety. In the same breadth, some of my friendships have borne pain, scars of betrayal and emotional turmoil.*
- *It's okay to grieve past relationships.*
- *Asking myself what kind of friend I am forced me to deeply reflect on how I show up in my friendships, my intentions, my values, and my efforts.*
- *At times, my reaction to situations within a friendship are often my inner child catastrophizing. I have learned that instead of being too quick to cut a friend off, I must ask, are those tears from the inner child within? If so, how can I attend to her?*
- *My friendships have helped me heal.*

We swapped our reflections and read them. Reading Zara's reflections was very insightful. On the one hand, I empathised deeply with some of her reflections. On the other hand, it emphasised that though difficult at times, adult friendships are necessary.

The older I become, the ability and opportunity to BE is something I crave for in my relationships. Probably because this is something I have struggled with for the most part. At one point, there was a tendency to bend or shift to fit in; to hold back or dim my light in some way, shape or form which was exacerbated in certain circles I found myself in. A lot of the times, I gave in.

For so long in some circles I found myself in, I felt that people did not know me fully. Truly…

This was very ironic because I was the go-to person. It's not something I take pride in but it was the truth. In some instances, it was partly because I was not given the space to be.

In most of the other instances, it was because I struggled to let people in completely. 'Will I be accepted? What if I'm *too much* for them?'

I also had trust issues – not trusting people enough with vulnerability. As a result, I became a master of giving people parts and truths about me without actually giving them ME. It was easier to tell people about myself than it was to open up my heart and let them in. This created the semblance of intimacy without true intimacy. I was honest but held my heart close to myself.

Little did I know that I was doing myself a disservice. Counter dependence fostered loneliness and isolation within.

Vulnerability calls for a total revealing of my emotions and weaknesses. It means telling the people I trust how I genuinely and truly feel, no matter how difficult it may be. It means telling people how they made me feel – good and bad, what I expect from them, and how I would like to be loved or supported.

I was better at creating such space for others *than* I was receiving it.

I knew I had to get better at being vulnerable.

The truth is there is no shortcut for cultivating healthy honest bonds or growing a thriving community other than this.

Do I still think it is a risk? Of course! We humans can be fickle and sometimes not everyone has the capacity to meet ones' vulnerability with warm embrace. However, is it a risk worth taking? Absolutely! As a relational being, deep down, I want to be seen, accepted and truly supported. That cannot happen outside of being vulnerable. Besides, there will be people equipped to handle my heart with care.

I would come to know this because of friends like Zara.

Our friendship is one I cherish so much. I have grown to *be* in it. We've had healthy conflicts and I am able to be vulnerable and genuinely speak my mind and vice versa.

I know there is still much growing and learning to be birthed from our friendship as we experience more of life but, right now, I am grateful for such a safe space.

Adult relationships can be hard but *I can do hard things* too.

In navigating adult friendships, I am learning about myself which in turn helps others to understand me as well.

9.

Embracing Conflicts

"I don't understand how you could say that you do not feel heard by me. That really hurt me," Nneka lamented.

This was during a difficult conversation we had the day before. I had expressed that I didn't feel as supported by her as a friend. I was honest in my delivery but genuinely was not intentionally trying to hurt her feelings in the process. Sometimes, the truth is bitter regardless of how it is delivered. This was not the first time we were having a difficult conversation. We openly discussed our hearts with each other and I apologised for how my words may have hurt her. We talked things out and came to a healthy conclusion. This made us closer.

I never thought I would be the one to say this, but that conversation made me appreciate 'conflict'. It challenged the way I perceived it and sparked a desire to embrace it. It also made me realise that I am growing.

I had been posed with similar instances where I had not dealt with conflict this way. Usually, I would abruptly cease communication with whoever I am in conflict with, without reason for my disappearance, or would withdraw myself in conversations and go mute. Passive aggressive in some instances. When it came to any kind of confrontation or conflict, I was extremely avoidant, and in many cases, I didn't like the vulnerability that came with the conflict.

However, my relationship with Nneka's few 'conflicts' made me realise that *healthy* conflict can be good and should not be something I shy away from. It is okay to have uncomfortable conversations –be it with myself, loved ones, at work; you name it. Even with that, I am learning to be open to receive feedback, possibly backlash at times from these uncomfortable situations without being defensive or internalising it. We humans are complex and some responses I might receive may not be exactly what I want to hear, but having the wisdom to accept criticism objectively is the key.

Additionally, I learnt to accept that sometimes, I can be the *villain* in other people's stories too. I was (unintentionally) in this scenario. That makes me human. I acknowledge it, take accountability, apologise and make amends where necessary. That definitely is easier said than done, at times.

Conflict, if done well can lead to positive outcomes. I say *done well* because conflict can definitely be done wrong. Like the conflict between Mama Emeka and Mama Obi.

Mama Emeka and Mama Obi went at loggerheads during the women's August village meeting in 2008. In 2008, mama took me to this annual meeting. These meetings were an avenue for women in the community, both home and abroad to come together to bond and discuss opportunities for the betterment of the community.

From what I gathered, Mama Emeka and Mama Obi were friends, although that didn't seem like it during their altercation.

It started during the meeting's intermission. The first session of the meeting had concluded and it was time for the women to have a break. There were usually refreshments shared at the meeting: jollof rice, small chops*, drinks like malt, beer, and some water.

Once the Chair of the meeting, Lady Ugorji announced it was time for refreshments, Mama Obi says out loud in the presence of all in attendance:

"Mama Emeka, why don't you serve the refreshments for everybody?" in what was not only a sarcastic but condescending tone.

"I don't understand. Why me?! Someone else can do it! You nko, can't you do it?!", Mama Emeka retorted. From her tone, it was clear she was either upset about being singled out to serve or at the tone at which the ask was delivered, or both.

"Ah ahn. Calm down now. It was only a question! Besides, are you not the youngest in our group? Why can't you serve us?", Mama Obi pushed.

For someone who claimed to be Mama Emeka's friend, Mama Obi woefully failed at reading her friend's body language and honestly, respecting her boundaries at the first instance.

"Mama Obi, don't you dare tell me to calm down. Who do you think you are?! Let me tell you, respect is reciprocal", her tone definitely had more tempo in it this time.

Instead of Mama Obi to take accountability there and then and apologise for any miscommunication or hurt caused, she didn't.

I guess she took offence at the way her dear friend responded and before everyone knew it, they both started hurling insults at each other. Things almost got physical…

Both women were separated to cool off at individual ends of the compound where the meeting was held. It took another extra 30 minutes for the meeting to resume after that.

Everyone including mama couldn't believe how that escalated quickly (and why it did.) It was clear that perhaps there might have been some unresolved issues between the two friends *beforehand* which potentially amplified the current situation.

I'm reminded of that situation as an example of conflict done wrong. The lack of accountability, willingness to listen and respect for each other were some markers for this. Also, the potential avoidance of prior issues between the two of them was another marker.

I wondered why Mama Obi took offence to Mama Emeka expressing her disapproval on her insistence of serving. How that presence of 'conflict' or 'confrontation' by expressing disapproval can be interpreted as *disrespect* (no matter how it is done) especially in that cultural context.

Embracing conflict is still difficult to do, but the more I engage in and with 'conflict,' the more I get used to how uncomfortable it is and the better at it I become.

Adaora's Adulting Chronicles

"Conflict has the ability to change you and your relationships, Adaora. It is an opportunity to express your desire to feel respected and to ascertain if the other person values the relationship in a similar manner. It is also an opportunity to know the other person better." Another Dr. Kari gem.

I had expressed how difficult it was for me to engage in conflict and how my entire existence was literally in flight-mode the minute I could perceive any type of conflict looming.

She highlighted how conflict requires vulnerability and wondered if that was something I was running away from.

Of course, it was…

The willingness to let myself be seen has always been a challenge. An ironic challenge at that because I deeply craved to be seen and known.

"Vulnerability. Ownership. Communication. Acceptance. Boundaries. These are key pillars of conflict management" she added.

On acceptance in relation to conflict, I am learning that conflict does not always go well. Like Mama Emeka and Mama Obi almost giving us a WWE show at that meeting!

Sometimes, even with the right intentions and approach in engaging with conflict, people's reactions differ and that's okay. Mama Emeka being triggered by Mama Obi's expression of disapproval at her comments, is an example of that.

This is a tough pill to swallow as a recovering people-pleaser, but I am willing to make peace with it. I am not in control of other people's reactions and cannot keep wearing guilt like a badge of honour.

PART III

This is a lot.

10.

Grief

"But Adaọra, you know for us death is not the end," a colleague of mine reassured me. She was a Christian and that was her response after I told her about the death of an aunty of mine. She was not wrong but, in that moment, it was hard to believe…

As a Christian, I believe it to be true that although death seems final, it is not completely the end for people who believe in Jesus. However, it does not take away the hurt of losing someone – of realising you won't physically see that person again. All you are left with are memories…

Death has a way of teaching and reminding me about the fragility of life – a lesson I am not sure I have completely learnt, even though I have experienced a few deaths close to home.

Papa Nnukwu's death was close to home. He was mama's father. Mama was his first daughter. It was devastating when he passed. His death came as a huge shock to the family; it's hard to even think about it. I was still at home in Nigeria when it happened. It was tough for mama. I loved him so much and he loved me.

Whenever I was around him, he always made space for me. Sharing his food with me, asking about how I was finding school and indulging me with all his historic stories including tales of his survival of the Nigerian Biafran war. I miss his humour, his wisdom, his experience, his heart to give, his charisma, his love for family and unity. I miss him calling me "nne m" – that was his name for me. "Nne m" means 'my mother.'

According to him, I reminded him of his mother, and he believed that I was his mother reincarnated. A true peacemaker at heart. So much, so that he was awarded a title of Ome Udo* 1 of his village. A title that validated this attribute of his.

Papa Nnukwu was adept at managing conflicts and arranging peace-making meetings. I recall many memories of being greeted by an influx of people in his living room (most times when we visited), who came to benefit from his expertise. A true man of integrity; respected and revered. Even the *Igwe** of the village sought his counsel. A wise man. Ugh. I wish he lived longer but he lived well. Gone at the ripe age of 97 – a celebration of life.

Another one – Pa Tobias. When Pa Tobias (Papa's father) died, I was not told. I was at university writing my second-year exams. Mama and Papa thought it best not to break the news to me until I had finished my exams. Coincidentally, I was travelling back home to visit them afterwards.

Unbeknownst to me, they had fixed the funeral around the time so I could be present for it. Unfortunately for everyone, a distant family relative accidently broke the news to me – *"Good afternoon, Adaora; we are really sorry to hear about your grandad's passing. Please accept my condolences. We will endeavour to be at the burial in the village"*.

My eyes met this WhatsApp message notification with confusion because it's been years since I spoke with this person. My confusion was then followed by an overwhelming sense of anxiety. I could not believe what I was reading. Rushing out of the restroom at university, I immediately made a call to Mama. I'm not sure why but the tears started falling as her line began to ring. She picked up and I immediately asked – "Is Mpa dead?!" She could sense the fear and sadness in my voice. The call went silent. I just knew…

"Who told you?!" mama asked with so much frustration in her voice. I started to cry even harder. Everything else she said was a blur. How could Papa die now? I was going to travel in a few weeks' time to see everyone at home including him. I was excited to see him. I bought him some nice shirts and looked forward to seeing the pride on his face that his granddaughter had bought him things from *obodo oyibo**.

I was close with Papa before *japa*. We regularly visited the village to see him, so forming this bond was somewhat inevitable. He was strong. Although he had a bad stroke towards the end of his life, he fought so well against it. I looked forward to him being here for a while – to see me achieve some milestones such as graduating from university and even getting married.

When I eventually arrived at the village, I could not stop crying. Witnessing and being part of the funeral process was not easy, but we made through it. I don't know how Papa did it.

I miss Pa – his laugh, his charisma and love for storytelling amongst other things. Although Pa was frugal, he was rich. Hindsight is such a gift because looking back now, I can see how rich he was. A farmer at heart, yet he owned multiple farms and palm plantations which produced gallons of palm oil and kernel to trade annually. He also reared chicken and goats at some point. Pa was actually a *baller*. Although, I couldn't tell you where all that money went, apart from reinvesting in the business and his children, I loved Pa's business mindset.

Just like mama's, Pa was also charismatic. He was sought after for counsel. With his snuff (tobacco) in hand ready to be launched into his nostrils, he would dish out counsel to his visitors in his *Obu**. He was also revered at his local catholic church.

Another death close to home was Uncle Dike. A family friend and Papa's close friend.

"E bere m akwa o {I cried o} and it really affected me, but I'm okay now,"* Papa said on the phone when I called to check on him after receiving the news. His statement was followed by a brief silence. A silence which was loud enough to echo that this was still very fresh for him and he probably still was not okay – he couldn't have been. His not so brief silence was followed by a very deep sigh.

Death is painful. Uncle Dike's death was a painful one. It was yet another abrupt passing. This conversation I had with Papa happened a few days after his funeral. I had called to check in and find out how it went since I was not present. It was clear that Papa was still grieving. Family, friends and loved ones alike.

"This life" he said followed by another pause. Papa had never been the

one to admit his feelings – an observation very common amongst older Nigerian men, if not the majority of them, both young and old. He has always been the strong one, the resilient one, the one who didn't leave much room to feel – even when grandpa (Papa's father) died, he seemed to be fine and carried on like it was a normal cycle of life. In his defence, the numerous cultural responsibilities that fell on him as a man of the house with things to sort out during the funeral preparation gave him less room to feel.

This time, it was different. He was vulnerable and admitted how he genuinely felt – a rare occasion which left me feeling sorry for him. He had just lost a dear friend…

They had been friends for many years and both our families did life together for the most part. I spent a significant amount of my childhood growing up with Uncle Dike's children. Both our families lived in the same neighbourhood for most of my childhood, so this friendship preceded my birth.

It is scary to acknowledge that grief is a part of life. Whether it is grieving situations or what could have been or the loss of people in our lives who are alive, or loved ones who are no longer with us here. It sucks.

When I got off the phone with Papa, I could not help but wonder about the thoughts in his mind; the ones he didn't communicate. Was he thinking about his own death? Uncle Dike was a few years younger than Papa; death is no respecter of age; could this have been playing on his mind too?

His vulnerability during that last conversation was refreshing, but it gave me a slight concern about his wellbeing. I continued to check in as much as I could as he navigated his own grief.

I find it hard to have conversations around grief.

"It is well." "I'm so sorry!" "Praying for comfort." As kind and gentle as they sound, these statements do not always seem to suffice. It feels very insufficient for such an experience of loss. I generally struggle with the right words to say when someone is bereaved. This confusion isn't absent if I am the one grieving – I usually don't always know what or how to feel.

Grief can be uncomfortable. It requires one to tarry in a way. Perhaps because there is no set expiration date on it and it differs for everyone. You cannot rush the process so most times, you have to sit with it – and that can be uncomfortable...

Grief can also magnify life as unfair too. When an aunt of mine passed in our family, it felt like our world came crashing down. And it did, in that moment. For the next person however, their world was perfectly fine. I remember having pockets of anger about this reality. I wanted the rest of the world and time to stop for me and my family to process and navigate yet another loss, but that didn't happen.

Life went on; life goes on. In fact, on the same day the news regarding my aunty's passing came, a friend of mine was throwing a get-together with her loved ones to celebrate her birthday, and I couldn't go.

I saw some clips on social media as joy radiated from the videos and her beautiful tribe who celebrated her life. As much as that was a good and beautiful thing to see and watch, it just didn't seem fair that life was not waiting for us to recover or even pause to grieve. For me, that has been one of the most difficult things about grief. Balancing the fact that grief has no expiration date on this side of life, yet acknowledging and navigating life as it goes on.

As much as I have experienced a few deaths close to home, I still get moments of anxiety when thoughts of potential deaths happening, cross my mind. Sometimes, I cannot even fathom them! I get really scared about how it might change me and how painful it will be. Would I even cope? Sometimes, I think about my own death too…

"I have a feeling that I am going to die young," Zara told me as we sat in front of the beach, having a picnic that same hot summer at Margate. Her

eyes met my confused eyes with much conviction.

I immediately gave the response of a typical devoted Nigerian mum – *"God forbid!"*. Then proceeded to probe even further on why she would think to say such a thing. She explained that she truly believed it and had a strong conviction about it. Although I saw this statement as not only a negative thing to happen, but to profess, Zara thought otherwise.

She went on to explain how this conviction had given her a sense of urgency to live life more intentionally. It made her become more present in her relationships and give herself wholeheartedly to people through her service to them. It made her invest in her craft, talents and pretty much anything she found her hands doing.

Who would have thought something so morbid could channel such inspiration?

Suddenly in that moment as she explained, I could see how this strong conviction manifested in Zara's life – everything she highlighted from her perspective, she practiced. Zara was intentional; she is the one friend who would ask from time to time on the best way she could support her friends.

She would celebrate my wins, no matter how small they were. She is the friend who loves loudly. She consistently looks for opportunities to serve the people in her life. She follows all her many passions in terms of talents as though there was indeed no more time and had to give an account for them one day. She tries to stay present in any given moment.

This revelation from Zara challenged me. It was sobering to hear.

If I lived my life with the constant consciousness that death was lurking around the corner, how differently would I live it? How intentional would I become?

If I lived my life as though it was a loan to steward and account for, how differently would I live it?

11.

Unpacking Trauma

Trigger warning

I tend to internalise a lot. Through therapy, it was highlighted to me that my tendency to continuously do this is most likely a trauma response.

At the time of discovery, I did not know what internalising meant. I did not have the language for it. I came to find out from the resources I was given that it is the *"the unconscious mental process where characteristics, beliefs, feelings and attitudes of other people are assimilated into your own self, which can lead to serious damage to ones' overall mental health, self-esteem and relationships with others."* [11]

My default resolve when things didn't go to plan or when people reacted negatively towards me was feeling the need to take responsibility that it had something to do with me. I also internalised their opinions of me and would take these negative reactions on myself through negative self-talk by default, constantly taking the blame for other people's reactions even when it had nothing to do with me.

Trauma: "The physical, emotional and psychological response to a distressing event or experience. It's a deep wound from past events that affects how we perceive and experience the present and anticipate the future. It is any moment or series of moments that have negative lasting impact on our identity, perception and reality" [Book: Why am I like this? How to break cycles, heal from trauma and restore your faith by Kobe Campbell][14].

For a long time, it took me a while to acknowledge that what I went through was trauma. Especially because I thought *it wasn't that bad.* Somehow, acknowledging that I went through trauma felt like I was ungrateful (especially as some of the roots were tied to my moving away from home in childhood). Afterall, I was abroad and was privy to opportunities some of my mates weren't; what could possibly be traumatic about that? How could I complain?

Somehow, the mere fact of acknowledging trauma felt like I was complaining. I felt guilty to acknowledge and process all I had gone through because it felt like a privilege to do so. In a sense, perhaps it was. I guess not everyone has the opportunity to be in an environment that grants them space for that. Some people I know are in environments that solely forces them to focus on survival.

I also felt guilty for acknowledging and processing my trauma because on the surface-level, I came across as someone who '*had it all together*.' I feared the reaction I would receive when I eventually admitted that, I in fact, did not have it altogether, and the only reason people thought this was because they never actually *saw* me, nor took the chance to really get to know me.

The fact that I was so counter dependent was because I felt like I had no choice, as most people around me automatically assumed I was fine and did not need any help. Perhaps this was because I masked things well? Perhaps, it was because I knew how to carry on regardless…

Perhaps, it was because I'd been let down in the past and that was the only way I knew how to cope? I was over-correcting.

"*Who told you what you went through wasn't that bad and why do you believe that?*" Dr. Kari challenged me at one of our therapy sessions. I had chills. I paused. Her further response after I found the words to reply to the striking question was the release I needed:

"*Just because it's not that deep for others, does not mean it isn't for you. Trauma impacts and shows up differently in everyone. Don't use someone else's experience as a yardstick to define the validity of your trauma. Pain is pain; do not rationalise or invalidate how you feel and the impact of what you have experienced.*"

Just wow!

<u>You cannot heal what you can't acknowledge</u>

It is fascinating that I thought the emotional neglect, bullying, loss of close friendships, experiences of betrayal, *japa*/moving around a lot as a child and… sexual abuse was not that deep. I had unconsciously trivialised what many would consider *deep* experiences in fact.

Like how the bullying at my new school after I left home chipped away at my confidence. How having to adapt to a new environment exacerbated my otherness. Or how moving around a lot and having to make new friends afresh meant that for a long time, I struggled with a sense of belonging. Or how no longer having my mama emotionally and physically present meant I suppressed my feelings, so I do not come across as a 'burden'.

For a long time, I even repressed my experiences of being sexually abused at the tender age of 12. Till this day, I struggle to remember all the details of it. All I know was on that faithful day, I was home alone with someone who was supposed to be my guardian. Mama and Papa had left for a function. Michael Jackson's "remember the time" was playing on TV (for a long time, I couldn't listen to this song the same way). Before I knew it, I was on the bed with someone whom I trusted, on top of me.

I didn't know what or how to make sense of the act. I was filled with so much terror to tell anyone about it. One of the main feelings I felt as a result was so much shame. A huge fraction of that shame was because this abuse was more coercive than forceful. Unfortunately, at that age, I heard about rape and from what I heard, it was usually a forceful act. But this wasn't – so what was this? Surely, it must have been my fault because it was not forceful, and I did not resist? Instead, I complied. Yet another thing I internalised...

It took me time to realise that:

1) Just because it wasn't forceful, does not negate the fact that it **was** abuse.

2) I was a minor under the supervision of someone at the cusp of adulthood; an eighteen-year-old boy who took advantage of me – none of what happened was my fault.

All these traumatic experiences sowed seeds within me. The interesting thing about trauma is that it does not ask for your permission to sow them. These seeds then created patterns which became more evident the older I got – suppressing my feelings, people pleasing, extreme self-reliance (counter-dependence) amongst others. It also distorted my perception about the way I saw myself, reality and even how I viewed and related with God. Constant feelings of unworthiness, trust issues, and the inability to receive love were some testaments to the effect of those seeds sown.

A chunk of adulting so far has been spent unearthing different types of traumas through therapy, with God and within my community. Being in a community has a great way of revealing areas of previous hurts that need addressing. For someone who had trust issues with people, it took some time to get accustomed to the reality that though some of the hurt I held on to was caused by others, I also needed people, to heal from them too.

Gaining an understanding of the mind through various mediums such as therapy, podcasts, books, and interviews helped give language to my experiences.

Above all, knowing God for myself, finding and receiving my identity in Him has helped tremendously! Rediscovering my identity in God has been pivotal, especially as it had been very easy to hold unto trauma like a crutch. Sometimes, it felt easier to stay the victim and not take responsibility for my healing because healing felt too tasking.

The trauma felt like it was taking on its own identity in me and almost became like a 'comfort zone'. Knowing God allows me to separate my identity from trauma. It is not *my* trauma. I am not what happened to me! Yes, what happened to me left patterns, but ultimately, they do not define me.

This allows me to graciously embrace the work of healing with a confidence that ultimately, I am who God says I am. This has been particularly key in moments when it feels like the work of healing is never-ending; where new patterns of negative behaviour surface, and I question whether all the previous work done has been futile. On those days, my brokenness magnifies itself and I wonder why I am so broken? I hold on to my *true* identity – I am eternally made, loved, known and valued by God.

"*Pace yourself.*" Dr. Kari would always remind me. "*Trauma can be acute and a build-up of everyday wounds. It took time to happen and crystallise patterns within you; it'll take time to unlearn,*[14]" she would repeat.

She knew I had a tendency of being so hard on myself…

The journey of healing is a long, messy, yet necessary one. So, although I may not be responsible for what happened to me, I am responsible for healing and that does take intentional work and effort. But I know I do not have to do this work alone. Ultimately, God is even more committed to my healing too, and it has been freeing, sitting, and processing all the whirlwind of emotions and realisations of unpacking with Him.

Having said that, I wish healing didn't take so long and wasn't so painful at times. Alas, it is not how it works and as expected… all those years of conditioning cannot be undone overnight.

One of the books I read, shed some insight as to why most times, it can be difficult to undo or change negative patterns caused by trauma, especially in relation to our human biology. Apparently, trauma changes the wiring of the brain; it went something along the lines of highlighting that there are neurological pathways within our brains created to hold unto patterns, and each time a new thinking or pattern is introduced, a neurological pathway is formed.

Repetition of thinking (which includes words we hear or the stories we tell ourselves) strengthens the wiring of that neurological pathway which then manifests and is grounded in behavioural patterns. Crazy!

Therefore, to counter that, a new thinking or pattern will need to be introduced and repeated to re-wire that pathway in the brain.

"*Be transformed by the renewing of your mind*" – a latter part of a Bible verse in Romans 12:2 I had known, rang so true in that moment of reading this part of the book. Suddenly, it made so much sense!

I pondered on this discovery for a long time. Dare I say it flipped a switch in my mind and explained why unpacking trauma felt like such work and effort. It is…

It also challenged me because in that moment, I began to recall the many words and patterns of thinking from others and myself that were not true but had made their home in my mind and deeply rooted in my actions. Reading that made me realise even more why I had to give myself grace and patience on this journey of healing. It also gave me the zeal to be more intentional about telling myself stories rooted in truth, instead of the lies I had repeated to myself.

Unpacking the trauma that happened to me has an interesting way of making me notice patterns of trauma in others too. As I unpack mine, I begin to psychoanalyse others as well. Like maybe Aunty Adaego found it difficult to be emotionally present because she was also neglected, seeing as she was a child to parents who were separated? Perhaps she had an identity crisis having been born to parents from different races? Did she face some kind of abuse? Who knows...

Seeing the patterns in others and trying to connect their dots has been somewhat helpful to me in giving them some grace for their actions that hurt me, even though it doesn't always lessen the hurt or pain caused.

A huge part of unpacking some of the things I had experienced was *acceptance*. Accepting that unfortunately, things happened the way they did and there is nothing I can do to change the past. As painful as acceptance can be, it helped me to no longer remain stuck in the past – spending energy wishing and hoping that things went differently and resenting others for the things they did or did not do…

Instead, it has given me room to let healing in.

12.

Navigating Romantic Relationships

Emeka was my first crush. The heart skipping so fast not to miss a beat-type crush. The palms sweaty and stuttering whenever we got to speak in class-type crush…

I was in secondary school then in Nigeria. He was tall, light skinned, neat (his uniforms were always well ironed). He also had a little *swag* to his walk. This attraction was all physical and it turned out I was not the only girl in school he had this effect on. I eventually found out the feeling was in fact mutual, and that did a whole lot of boosting for my ego.

My crush with Emeka never really blossomed to anything serious though. Partly because he gave off the impression that he wanted to be chased. He loved the attention that came with being one of the *hottest* boys that year in school; it definitely got to his head and I can't blame him for that.

My second crush after Emeka was Paul, two years later after Emeka in the same school. Again, handsome, light-skinned (I probably had a type back then), an eye-candy for sure. The ladies loved him too. This time though, Paul was not in the same class as me. He was a few years above me as he was my senior.

As a result, our paths never directly crossed i.e., we never really spoke until I left the school. So, I crushed from afar. A couple of years after I had left the school and relocated to the UK one unexpected evening, I received a friend request on Facebook from Paul.

At first, I thought it was a *catfish*, but I came to find out that it was not. To say I was shocked would be an understatement. I accepted the friend request with great anticipation. With bated breath, I waited for him to message me because messaging him first felt desperate. He eventually messaged.

From the first conversation, we got on like a house on fire. Talking and chatting into midnight as the days progressed. As a naïve youngster, I wasted no time in beginning to imagine my future with him; daydreaming about our wedding – what are the odds that someone I crushed on from afar in school, years later will find me and add me on Facebook? We started talking and got on so well. Surely, this was a sign that it was meant to be; this was fate…

At the time of what seemed like a God-ordained connection to me, I was in the UK, and he had relocated to France with his family. In one of our frequent conversations then, he mentioned how this distance between us was not ideal and longed for the day we were going to be together. He was thinking of moving to the UK to further his education, so the prospects of this becoming a reality were high at the time. The distance didn't really matter though; I was so optimistic and willing.

Things were going well; we carried on speaking consistently for almost a month and a bit, until I expressed that I really liked him. And then, crickets. I was ghosted – so much for shooting my shot…

I was confused, perplexed and infuriated at the sudden silence of his. Follow up text messages, long paragraphs later… nothing. No response. By this point, we had already graduated our chats from good old Facebook to WhatsApp. I even tried to call, but nothing either…

I was so heartbroken. I didn't know what to do.

I poured my heart out to a close friend at the time who was infuriated on my behalf. She grabbed my phone, drafted yet another long but frank paragraph; this time, expressing the frustration I had regarding his silence. To which he then, finally, replied: *"Ok"*.

I could not believe my eyes. I stared at the response in utter disbelief. After almost three weeks of radio silence, that was the fitting response he could come up with?! I honestly wasn't sure which was more heartbreaking; his ghosting or nonchalance to how I genuinely felt. For someone who I was not in a relationship with yet, the heartbreak was intense – I was grieving my unmet expectations and what could have been yet again.

Adaora's Adulting Chronicles

A few years later and it has still been an interesting journey of trying to navigate romantic relationships. This has most likely influenced my current sentiment on dating.

I now find the whole idea of 'dating' a bit cringe. I'm not sure what it is exactly but the thought of telling more than a few potential partners about my favourite colour and where I see myself in the next five years is hilarious to me. It feels a bit performative as well – why do I need to *sell* myself? I feel the same way about job interviews to be honest, but that's neither here nor there. However, I do think getting to know people can be beautiful too – how ironic.

I do love, love. I love the idea of partnership and commitment within a relationship. And a healthy, safe, secure, and Godly relationship is something I desire.

Exactly 48 days to my 25th birthday, I was reflecting on my life. Birthdays for me the older I get tend to be quite sober (a little too sobering sometimes). On this occasion, I was particularly reflecting on my experiences with romantic relationships (or lack thereof) thus far, and why it had seemed to be a *struggle*.

None of my few experiences of dating or getting to know someone had materialised into an actual relationship. It's either I like someone, and it is not reciprocated, or someone likes me, but the feeling isn't mutual from my end, or we both don't complement each other. I had found myself in a few situationships; *let's see how things go kind of relationship with nothing defined.*

Leading up to my birthday, I had yet another interesting experience which exacerbated this reflection. It was a hilarious encounter with someone who was interested in me.

"*If you tell me you are in a relationship, I will not slap you. Someone appreciating you is not a sin and the way you blocked me shows no sign of maturity*" read a snippet of the text message from Mr. T…

Mr. T and I met at a family friend's function for the first time. Prior to that, I did not know who he was, and had not heard about him either. At the function, we barely had a proper conversation; we spoke here and there but nothing in depth. When he was about to take his leave, he requested for my number. Initially, I was apprehensive (partly because I sensed what was coming and I did not want it) but also because I felt we hadn't built enough connection at the function to warrant my number.

My people-pleasing self was struggling to say no at the time, as I did not want to come across as rude or offend him and so, I obliged. A couple of days later, he messaged me on WhatsApp professing his *love* for me and immediately started talking about marriage. This was overwhelming for someone I had just met and did not know at all – a huge red flag for sure!

He spoke about how he had been observing me and thought I was a 'good fit for him'. Again, I had just met the guy; I had never met him prior to the function, so I was confused as to how, when and where this observation was happening – how can one come to such conclusion from a function with no proper conversation or interest to get to know me first, or enquire if this is something I am in fact interested in at all?

I clearly and politely declined Mr. T's offer. Other than the fact that his approach was a huge turn off, I genuinely wasn't interested from the get-go. Mr. T was insistent – bombarding me with messages upon messages and calls once at 11:57pm to reconsider his proposal! I ignored them all initially, but they continued. I reiterated to him that I was not interested in what he was proposing – that I marry him. Then came another long paragraph with contents that rubbed me off the wrong way. At that point, I had enough and proceeded to blocking him on WhatsApp.

A few days later after he must have noticed that was the case, he sent me an enraged text message which included the snippet above. I was shocked when I saw it because it didn't occur to me that he could still reach me via text, even though I blocked him on WhatsApp. Asides everything he said in his message, I found it fascinating he assumed that I declined his advances because I was in a relationship when I blatantly refused his advances because I just was not interested in the proposal, nor impressed with his approach.

Being in a relationship seemed to make logical sense to him as reason for me to reject his offer. I was not. Anyways, after I read the message, I proceeded to block his number on everything else so he could not reach me. I genuinely did not have the capacity to entertain this any longer and whatever that was turned into harassment and so, I called it quits again for peace of mind.

Dating is truly an interesting ride – I've met some *unique* characters along the way…

Although the incident with Mr. T was not my fault, it got me thinking about my experiences with romantic relationships in general. I wondered whether anything was wrong with me. Were my standards too high? What even were my standards? I began to ponder on why I had not been in a serious relationship thus far.

The truth was, it wasn't my standards – they were valid and reasonable, but I was letting my experiences make me second guess what I wanted.

My desire of being in a relationship has fluctuated over the years. I obsessed over this desire. At other points, I wanted nothing to do with the idea of being in a relationship. At 25, I was tired. Tired of thinking about anything to do with relationships which was even more tiring because it was (still is) a recurrent topic of discussion; an *in-your-face* kind of topic which can be annoying at times. I feel like there is so much emphasis on romantic relationships and on marriage. In an unhealthy way at times – perhaps because of the level of importance placed on it by society. It is heavily romanticised…

Having said that, I enjoy watching dating shows. I find them so entertaining! I once watched one which aimed to match and pair singles together based on how compatible their family and friends were. The single person who was searching for a potential partner would have to date the potential families of the different partners (three different families) first – it's called, *Date my Family (Nigeria).*

I loved the concept and approach to the show and though, there may have been some scripting involved, I enjoyed it. On one of the episodes, a bachelor who was looking for love in a potential date introduced himself. He said who he was, what he did and why he was on the show. He mentioned that *"he had been single all his life"*.

"How fascinating!" I thought. This was something that seemed peculiar to *just* me at the time, so it was somewhat comforting to hear. After his introduction, some of the families of potential partners he was dating were highlighted and they also introduced themselves. Once the introductions from the families were had, the narrator concluded the scene with these words: *"let's see if we can get this young bachelor out of his lifetime of loneliness!"*

I laughed in bewilderment. The bachelor said he was single all his life, not lonely all his life?! Those words implied that singleness equated to loneliness. Just because the bachelor had never been in a relationship meant he must have been lonely all his life…

Now, do I feel lonely sometimes in my singleness? Of course. I'd be lying to say that I didn't. However, equating singleness to a perpetual state of loneliness is a bit extreme. Afterall, anyone can experience loneliness… single or not. One can experience loneliness in other relationships. It is not something experienced only by single people.

Unfortunately, the narrative of singleness equating to being lonely and miserable is not an uncommon one. It is one of many that alludes to a deficiency and an incompleteness without a romantic relationship. It is one of the narratives that emphasise the idea that intimacy can't be found outside of a romantic relationship which I do not necessarily subscribe to.

"But you cannot have sex with your friends, can you?" I was once teased. The argument in this conversation was that sex was the highest form of intimacy; so how could I believe that I can form any intimate relationships outside of this? You know those conversations you have with someone, and it was clear that the person was not ready to hear what you were saying, but wanted to have the final say; so, you don't bother arguing? Yeah, this was one of them.

My whole point in that conversation was that it was limiting to believe that one cannot find intimacy and contentment outside of a romantic relationship – through other quality and meaningful relationships including relationships with God, friendships, and familial relationships. Both singleness and being in loving romantic relationships are gifts and should not be despised nor belittled. Equally, my worth is not tied to a relationship.

At 26, I decided to give the world of dating apps another try. I was encouraged to do so as the traditional route seemed to be yielding unfruitful results. I obliged and joined the infamous app 'Hinge.' It was another interesting journey to say the least.

I was not sure if it was the pool of people I was exposed to, but one observation was clear – there was general fatigue; apathy in some cases to dating. It was almost like everyone had seen *shege** and was tired of the dating scene. Some men I had encountered wanted to be wooed equally, if not more. It was really the ghetto in the streets…

Amidst, what most people might consider the 'perils' of dating, one thing it did for me was affirm the need to be self-aware, grounded, guarded and firm about what I wanted and to communicate those.

Dating has been revelatory for me – it has revealed and affirmed what is important.

I've met people that have tried to test my boundaries. Others, who have tried to make me second-guess the validity of my standards and some, who are just not on the same page as I am or have no idea about what they really want for themselves.

I've had to rethink what matters to me in view of the long term. It has made me come to a few realisations of not only how I want to be loved, but the pedestal I once placed on my ideal partner. Thanks to entertainment, film, music and social media, I had fallen into the trap of building some unrealistic expectations on what I wanted in a partner.

For example, as someone who used to want her partner to be her 'EVERYTHING,' I have come to realise that this puts a lot of pressure on one person who is as equally flawed as I am. It has made me realise the importance of having community even within a relationship.

Yes, I would like to have a friend in my partner, and I hope we are the best of friends, but I also need my other friends outside of that. Yes, I want my partner to be a safe space for me where I can be vulnerable and vice versa, and this is something I look out for in the process of dating. But I also have and need safe spaces outside of him – in my relationship with God, my friends, a mentor or possibly a counsellor or therapist.

Yes, I want to find some level of satisfaction in my partner, but I know and acknowledge that he cannot fulfil my every desire. It is only God that is inherently capable of that; true satisfaction comes from God.

In summary, I am still my own individual outside a partner.

These realisations have helped me put things into perspective and in turn, managed my expectations. This does not mean that I am advocating for settling or will settle for less. Rather, they are governed by the need to be aware and open about the realities of relationships. Relationships take work; mutual work.

On dating and the realisation of how I want to be loved, some of my personal reflections consist of the following:

- I want to be loved LOUDLY! – show me you love me and others that you love me. I want an active love; one that is not afraid to be seen.

- I want to be loved with intent – on one of my dating *escapades* someone who was interested in getting to know me asked to share my playlist with him. When I asked why, his response alluded to the fact that he would like to better understand who I am and believed an insight into what I listened to would spell some further connection. This gesture made my heart smile. I was mesmerised because it highlighted the genuine intent for me! Although it was unexpected, I loved it because of my passion for music. The attention to detail and commitment to know me in such a way was top tier. Sadly, the connection ended a couple of months later due to other reasons, but I still appreciated the time we spent getting to know each other. That gesture echoed his commitment at the time and painted a picture for me about some of the ways I would like to be loved, and for this, I am grateful for that man.

- I want to be loved with initiative and patience – Communicating my feelings and what I want can be difficult. This is an area of dating I am constantly challenged by. I've had to learn and still learning how to do this. Having said that, I love when people get it and when I don't have to constantly spell things out all the time. I love it when people show grace and are patient with me as I continue to grow in the ability to communicate my feelings.

- I want attention! – Although, this is something I constantly regulate because I can be overly obsessive which can be unhealthy, I tend to lose myself in a relationship as I desire to spend my time with someone I am romantically involved with. This was something I had to acknowledge in advance, and a goal I am mindful to keep watch of whilst navigating romantic relationships, is to ensure I don't negate my individuality. I want a partner who honours that too.

- I want to be loved with respect, kindness, care, and grace – with a biblical understanding of what love truly is and what the union of marriage represents especially in view of its sanctity. I want to be loved with commitment; one that shows up no matter what.

Outlining these desires of how I want to be loved feels quite weighty. Not in a way that I believe them to be impossible to fulfil, but in a way that sparks understanding that, I too, ought to be willing to put in the work to commit and honour the ways which my partner needs to be loved as well.

Anyways, from my lips to God's ears.

PART IV

The practical stuff

13.

Stewarding Finances

By the time I finished university, I had incurred about £2,000 worth of debt in overdraft.

Overdraft: "An arrangement via a bank that lets one borrow extra money through their current account. It is a form of debt and is repayable on demand. It can be arranged on unarranged. An arranged overdraft is when there is prior agreement to a limit on a current account that lets one spend a bit more money than one has. An unarranged overdraft is when one spends more money than they have in their account and has not previously arranged an overdraft limit with the bank. Both types of overdrafts have associated charges which will need to be paid if used." [12]

I opened a student account upon my entrance into school which came with an arranged overdraft of that amount. In hindsight, I'm not sure if taking this arranged overdraft was a wise decision. The temptation for the money (I technically did not have) was always there and before I knew it, I found myself in a situation where I spent all the money in the account, plus the entire overdraft.

To be fair, most of the expenditure was for valid reasons; however, if I managed and planned my finances better than I did, there would have been no need to use the overdraft, or at least, not use all of it. In other words, this was a classic example of; 'it's not you, it's me!' – it was not the overdraft; it was my finance habits.

Fast forward to a year later after university, I, or should I say, myself and my housemates who were friends, had unknowingly incurred about the same amount, if not more in council tax debt. Yikes!

Council tax: "A local taxation system used in England, Scotland and Wales. It is tax on a home; an annual fee (which is normally paid in monthly instalments), that the local council charges. This tax goes towards services provided by the local council such as rubbish and waste collection and disposal, police and fire services, libraries and education services, transport and highway services inc. street lighting and cleaning, road maintenance, environmental health and trading standards, administration and record keeping e.g. marriages deaths and birth, local elections, etc." [13]

In my second year of university, my friends and I decided to rent a house off campus as it was much cheaper than the campus accommodation. The entire experience was a learning curve, but among us, we split all the bills

– rent, water, electricity, broadband and sewage. As students, however, we were exempted from the council tax bill for the house, and had to send letters from our university to the council which stipulated that we were indeed, students.

After 3 years of study, we all graduated. However, 2 out of 4 of us moved out. We found replacements for them and this meant that we were not all students living in the house anymore. Unbeknownst to us, we were supposed to inform the council of this new change in tenant-ship (seeing as we were no longer students and were required by law to pay the council tax). Again, this did not occur to us…

A year and a bit later, when everyone was ready to move on to bigger and better things, we were contacted by the council through the post enquiring about the tenants in the house, highlighting records showed we were no longer students and were asked to confirm if this was true. Long story short, all the council tax bills we missed since the date of graduation were back dated and were asked to pay up! Unfortunately for us, we were moving house at the time, so this came in addition to the other final bills from the house.

And of course, this was all in addition to my £2,000+ debt too.

It was overwhelming!

It was such a frustrating time. I felt like I was constantly grappling with money. It seemed as if I was working, but had nothing to show for it. I could barely save, and I barely enjoyed the money I had, even when I had spare to spend on myself. I constantly worried about the next paycheck – would it be enough? What else could I do to offset all my debt? Could I save?

It was a lot…

My entire first year of working a *proper* job and the salaries that came from it was used to offset all my debts. I knew I had to make paying off my debt a priority, as being in such unnecessary debt made me uncomfortable. I just knew I had to do better with my finances.

I remember the day I finally paid off my debt like it was yesterday. Immediately, I paid the last instalment, I called the bank to close the entire account. Afterall, there was no longer a need for a student account, as I had a separate account to that one too. I did not also want the temptation of an overdraft present; an illusion of money I did not have…especially as I was yet to get my financial habits in check.

That evening, the lines to customer services were busy. After spending over 45 minutes on the telephone que, I decided to leave it until the next day. The following day, I made another call to customer services and eventually made it through to a call agent. During that phone call, I decided not to close the account entirely, but change it to a normal current account *without* an arranged overdraft.

"Would you like me to remove everything?" the agent asked in a bid to doublecheck if I wanted the entire overdraft removed.

"Everything!" I responded. My voice filled with so much certainty and excitement at the same time. A year later, since I formally started working, I was slowly getting rid of quite a lot of my debt and it was such a relief! The overdraft was the last debt to clear, and the last thing I wanted was an option to fall into that debt trap again.

(I still have my student loan debt to pay back of course, but that's okay as there is a system in place for the government to take directly from my paycheck).

Student loan: a scheme set in place by the UK Government for eligible students to borrow money and help them pay for university or college tuition fees. This loan is directly paid to the student's university of choice and attendance for the duration of study. However, it has to be paid back after graduation. Once the individual commences full-time employment, the money automatically starts getting deducted from the individual's pay once they hit a certain pay threshold. [5]

I felt accomplished and proud of myself for paying off my debt. It felt like I hit a savings target or even won the lottery! It was an accomplishment to stewarding my finances well.

Reflecting on how I felt that day made me realise how different individual and financial goals can be. For some, it could be to make six figures, but for me in that moment, it was paying off my debt, making a commitment to steward my finances well and applying it. My financial goals are exactly that; mine. Therefore, they should be realistic to my circumstances in each moment.

"Omo! Momsy and Popsy dey look me o. I gats get my money in order!" Edem, my tall, cheerful, Cross Riverian friend in his 30s, said in one of our conversations about money. This conversation echoed the very sentiments I had come to regarding my need for stewarding money well.

As he took another sip of water during our mid-conversation, he added: *"I have made peace with the fact that I do not come from a wealthy family, which means I gats hustle and use sense for my money. That one na my lot. Na so I see am, na so I go carry am!"* His pidgin English triggered so much nostalgia in me, whilst simultaneously bringing me to tears because I could relate with what he said.

Edem had moved to the UK at a latter part of his life to further his education. As expected, he stayed behind to settle in the country and *hustle*. Starting off as a carer during his studies, Edem hit the ground running in making sure he started earning a living in this new home of his.

He was raised by a widowed mother in Cross River State, Nigeria who literally sold most of her belongings to send him abroad just so he could have better opportunities to thrive. For Edem, making it was not an option; it was a necessity. There was no way he was going to let all his mother's sacrifices go to waste and she was literally depending on him for her daily bread.

Edem's story is both heartbreaking and inspiring. One for the books; I really hope he gets to tell it one day.

Both of us bonded over our unique but similar realities. Learning to steward our finances was not just a resolve we chose to come to; we *had* to. Life gave us no choice.

We bonded over the fact that each phone call from back home reminded us of how many financial responsibilities we had. We were frank about how although there wasn't direct pressure for this, the economic situation of things back home, coupled with our own internal pressures were enough pressure for us! Our prosperity was tied to their (our families) prosperity.

We made jokes from time to time which questioned *the* how and why we were not born into wealthy homes. How it would have been so convenient to not have such responsibilities. How it would be nice to be adopted by Dangote or Otedola; some of the elites from Nigeria.

As with most jokes, there's always some truth to it and this was no different. We were young, still figuring life out, working for our future family and children, plus our own goals, ambitions and dreams. That is enough pressure! Having to be financially responsible for our families on top of that can be a lot. But, like my very dear friend rightly pointed out, we have to make peace with our reality.

Edem's words came at the right time. I had started drowning in this sort of uncanny feeling of regret for where I was from. Where an incoming phone call from home gave me so much anxiety and would fill me with an immediate sense of overwhelm. My automatic sighs were evidence of this.

Where I began to see Mama and Papa as typologies for projects instead of human beings that deserved my support, nonetheless. Not just my financial support, but my emotional support too.

I needed that conversation and the multiple ones which followed suit.

Just like Edem, I am learning to accept my lot, instead of seeing it as a burden or something I have to do. I see it as something I *get* to do.

We get to support our own financially. As a result, we must take learning about money and stewardship seriously, because we cannot afford to be consistently careless with it.

Hopefully, changing the cycle of money in both our future families and giving our children the opportunity not to 'hustle' as much as we did.

Edem has taught me so much about finances. He shared how coming from a background like his made him so motivated by money, yet anxious of it. Enthused to continuously make more money to the point of being ridden with guilt about spending money on himself, and constantly being afraid that his money will run out, even with the more he made. He believed there were better things other than himself to invest his money in. He took *frugal* to another level.

Eventually, he admitted that although there is an importance of cutting one's *coat according to one's size*, such extreme ways of thinking robbed him off the joy of enjoying the fruit of his labour and it became unsustainable. He began to resent himself, everything, and everyone and that had to change.

"Discipline!" This was Edem's first response when I asked him what advice he would give his younger self on managing finances.

"Have discipline," he echoed. "I know the narrative nowadays is to earn more, but if you are not disciplined in the little, you won't be disciplined in much more."

He went on to explain how discipline helped him remove the sense of urgency to splurge without planning for things.

I was not surprised by his responses. Edem was indeed that guy – he had a spreadsheet to track and plan his finances. He knew where his money was going because he tracked every single transaction. He had plans for his money down to a T. He was proactive in his approach too – Edem could account for major plans for his money, even for the next five years. Literally! He saw saving and budgeting as an enticing competitive challenge against himself.

Therefore, if there was anything he wanted to accomplish with his money, big or small, he started way in advance to budget for it in order to meet his goals. As at the time of this conversation, he had already started saving towards a wedding and his future marriage, even though there was no girlfriend in sight, and he was ideally looking to settle down a couple of years later.

Talk about being proactive and…faith!

He also had what he described as an *emergency fund* – he had built enough savings to cover his current salary comfortably for six months if he lost or quitted his job. Again, talk about discipline!

He further explained that being proactive with his savings also gave him time to evaluate if he needed what he was saving up for, once his savings targets were met. On a few occasions, he found that once he reached the goal of what he had been saving for, he'd realise he didn't really need it, so he channelled the money to something more productive and beneficial.

"Give yourself grace and start with small changes. You can start with planning your finances monthly using the spreadsheet I gave," he encouraged.

He could tell I was beating myself up about the fact that I was yet to master my finances like him. He was quick to remind me that he didn't become the way he was overnight. It was through lots of trial and error. That was how he learnt. I couldn't expect to be like Edem and financially plan for the next 5 years when I was barely trying to be on top of my finances monthly.

Even though I still have so much more to learn about finances, I am grateful for my growth so far and I'm excited to grow even further. I'm thankful for friends like Edem who coincidentally became my teacher in this area, and has taught me the basics to budgeting, tracking and how to save. His budget spreadsheet has been a life saver so far.

If I was to answer the same question I posed to Edem – "What will you tell your younger self about finances?"

I will tell my younger self this: **"Find you an '*Edem*' – a friend, resources, a mentor, books, you name it, on finances as soon as possible. Then, start experimenting with whatever principles you have learnt and apply them sooner rather than later."**

Black tax was never a phrase I was familiar with, but soon enough, I became well-acquainted with it. I'd come to find out that it isn't as rare as I'd originally thought.

Nothing could have prepared me for the constant *billing.*

At times, I wondered if this was something I'd have to perpetually do for the rest of my life, considering the array of other increasing responsibilities that required money – food, clothing, toiletries, insurance, petrol, various other bills. You name it. There's always something that requires money.

Other times, I view black tax as a *privileged burden.* It kind of is.

On some occasions though, I questioned if I had the capacity to really be financially responsible for more? What happens when the kids start to come? Do I even want children? Because the ironic fact of this reality is that these financial responsibilities, do in fact increase.

I now understand that black tax does in fact come at varying degrees, and I'm slowly growing grateful for my lot.

I realise that I am in fact a beneficiary of black tax, and though it can be exhausting, it does benefit others too.

So, I've decided to not only accept my lot, but rest in it with wisdom, boundaries, and grace for myself and others too.

14.

To Chore or Not to Chore?

Doing laundry has an uncanny way of reminding me about the never-ending-ness of adulting. It feels like a metaphor for it.

I have a love-hate relationship with doing chores in general. Probably because for the most part, it felt like something I had to do and not something I get to do.

From as early as I can remember, I was indoctrinated into the world of domestics. My first task being to wash my school socks on my own as a little girl. In hindsight, I loved the initial task. I was glad Mama gave me permission that way to be like her. I washed those school socks time and time again from then on with so much joy; basking in the sense of independence that it brought me.

The older I got, doing chores not only increased, but became an expectation and necessity which was valid to some degree. However, that stripped away the joy I once had, especially in my new environment where it became a bit burdensome. It was always reiterated that it was my responsibility to consistently do the chores around the house. At times, I wondered whether I was in fact the maid or a member of the house.

I began to resent Jide as a result because he did not share the burden of doing chores with me once he became of age to. Every Saturday which was usually the 'big chore day,' I had to wake up bright and early to make my way through the list of chores, while he cosied up asleep in bed till midday.

No one had an issue with this as much as they would if the reverse was the case. He was a boy and according to cultural narratives, "it is the responsibility of the woman to keep and take care of a home" – and I had to accept that. The times I protested, that was the rebuttal I got.

My resentment grew because I didn't understand the logic behind that narrative. Aren't boys or men supposed to learn how to do these things too? Isn't Jide supposed to know how to cook? Isn't he supposed to be involved in the chores of the very house he lived in? Was it fair that I had to do ALL the chores?

No wonder Jide was clueless when he eventually got to university. His cluelessness became apparent to me the day when he called on the phone during his first week of university asking me how to make indomie noodles.

"Indomie!?"...

I'm sure he was not prepared for the thunderous laughter that ensued immediately after.

I could not believe my ears.

It was not his fault though. I guess you could say he was not given the opportunity to learn how to cook because everything was practically done for him at home. Now, the time had come for that to change.

Who knew that teaching Jide how to do chores would be an opportunity for us to bond.

Jide and I did not have the best of relationships. The resentment I had towards him made me unable to form a deeper emotional connection. Plus, he was a bit spoilt and entitled and I didn't have the energy to deal with that.

I was able to explain how to make indomie and other dishes to him over the duration of his course. He studied Architecture, so 7 years was a good enough time for him to learn and apply. A lot of what I did was sending him resources online and periodically guiding him through our video calls; no one has an excuse not to know how to cook with thousands of recipes on YouTube.

By the time he was done with university, he was a changed man. Even his mother was shocked!

Jide seemed to have a new perception of me, and likewise, myself towards him. We became closer and created safe spaces for each other.

I eventually expressed my resentment towards him all these years and he took it well and apologised. I could tell he was genuine. To my surprise though, he expressed that he also resented me to some degree. Apparently, he admired, but resented the way I seemed to 'have it all together'.

I was very independent and never seemed to need anyone, including him. He expressed that he felt inadequate next to me, and whilst this wasn't a thing I was conscious or deliberately aware of, that was how he felt. Thus, it led to a lot of his actions towards me including the lack of respect, disregard and in most cases, rudeness.

"Na wa!" was the echo in my mind. I couldn't help but wonder how all these years, *I* was the villain in Jide's story too…

I'm glad we were both able to let go of the past and was eventually open about it, no matter how painful it was. For so long, I held unto unforgiveness; wearing it like a badge of honour because it was valid. The truth is, it was too heavy, but I wouldn't admit it until I let it go.

Although I know how to do chores and I am grateful for how it was used by God as a vessel for restoration, I'm tired of it – tired of its never-ending-ness!

As a result, outsourcing things has become a new dream of mine. The goal now is to become financially capable to afford this – talk about redefining success.

15.

Productivity

The older I become, the more conscious I am about time. This consciousness has triggered the desire to start reading more about productivity and how to maximise the time I have.

A lot of content around productivity is tied to this 'hustle culture' and 'grind till you're dead' narrative or way of thinking which I found off-putting. Life is already tough, and I honestly do not need that kind of pressure.

However, I am aware that being productive (especially consistently) and sustainably is something I have struggled with. I also understand my need to get better in this area of my life.

Being accountable to myself can be difficult. Oftentimes, I set goals and do not meet them; thanks to habits like procrastination, under planning, overestimation or by plainly setting unachievable goals.

I've also found that my biggest, yet subtle culprit has been my inability to pivot in given moments. For example, setting an alarm to wake up at 6.00am, missing the alarm and waking up at a different time to the initial plan, and getting so disappointed at myself because I didn't stick to the original plan.

Instead of pivoting (adapting my original plan and moving things around), I choose to stay in my disappointment and automatically pronounce that day as ruined because one thing did not go to plan. Of course, my actions then reflected this, and I do in fact, end up not having a productive day when I *still* could have made the most of the time left and used it well. Even in moments where such disruptions in schedule might not be my fault, my reaction most times remained the same.

I didn't understand why my approach to productivity was like that for a long time.

In my quest to try and gain some understanding (and mastery if possible) on productivity, I began to do what was slowly becoming the bane of my adulting years – research; to learn more about this topic. I was tired of feeling like I was not utilising my time well and felt as if life were slipping through my hands.

Pivoting

Practically applying pivoting has been helpful. The idea behind this concept is being open to change or amending specific areas needed to continue reaching a desired goal. Using the example schedule earlier, to pivot will look like: missing my 6.00am alarm and waking up at 7.00am.

7.00am being the allotted time I had intended for my devotional and prayer for 1 hour, which should immediately follow by gym time.

Pivoting asks: "Could I still have prayer and devotional time but in 30 mins instead?" Or "Could I replace my gym time with that and move the gym later during the day?" – it seeks possible alternative scenarios or suggestions to allow daily goals to be met, still.

"Instead of feeling like a failure, can I still amend my time/schedule to accomplish the things I originally set out to do?" Of course, I could. Yes! It might not be in the duration of time I had planned, but these goals are still being met. It sounds simple or straightforward but, this is something I have had to train myself and my mind to commit.

I don't always get it right. There are days I still wallow in my disappointment or *woe is me* moments. However, I am actively learning to challenge myself and pivot. To challenge my thinking and approach, especially in moments when my schedule may not go exactly to plan.

The beauty about pivoting is that it helps me become more accountable to myself, which is ironic because the intent for creating a schedule in the first place is to be accountable. Me being upset for not meeting the schedule is also birthed from a desire to be responsible and accountable. However, wallowing in self-pity regardless of my initial intent is counterproductive. Therefore, learning to pivot makes more sense as it helps me to meet the overall goal of accountability.

Habit Stacking

"A book I would highly recommend is Atomic Habits by James Clear," Angela said at our first ever 1-2-1 meeting at work.

Atomic Habits, according to Angela was her most recommended book for people to read. After reading the book, I understood the hype. The interesting thing about the book is that everything the author shares is not necessarily ground-breaking, yet in many ways, it is.

Almost everything felt like it should have been *obvious* yet, the way it was broken down was very insightful.

Habit stacking was one of the principles the book explores to build new and healthier habits. The first step was to create a habit scorecard. I wrote down my habits I could think of, ranked them as positive, negative, or neutral habits (by putting a +, -, or =) sign next to them. This allowed me to see what habits I have, which of them are positive, i.e. pushing me to become the person I want to be, which of them are negative, i.e. deterrents, and finally, which of them are neutral, neither good nor bad. Doing this and putting my habits on paper allowed me to not only acknowledge them but become more aware of them.

It allowed me to try habit stacking, which is essentially introducing new habits in my routines by pairing them with habits I already do as a way to create a cue. Followed by writing out the intentions of habit stacking, whilst being specific with the timing and location too. Let's take a look at the following examples:

- *"After brushing my teeth in the morning, I will journal for 10 mins."*
- *"Whilst having breakfast, I will read 10 pages of my fictional novel."*
- *"Before I have my lunch in the afternoon, I will do some pilates for 15 mins."*
- *"After I turn off my 7.00am alarm, I will spend time with God for 20 mims."*

This way, the brain uses the former automatic habits as a cue for new ones. In exploring this principle, James explains the importance of being specific with these habit intentions utilising time and location. He explains the importance of making them achievable to start off with, then building momentum and small increments as time goes on. That way, it is more sustainable and achievable which will in turn encourage one to keep going.

I experienced this first hand with setting an intention of building a habit to working out or moving my body consistently. For months, my goal was to work out or move my body for *just* 15 mins. Initially, when I set that, I thought it was ridiculous because I knew that I could push myself further.

However, I followed the author's principle. This meant that I *remained* consistent to my goal and have been able to push myself beyond the limit. Even on the days where I feel weak, I can still meet my goal because of how achievable it is, which in turn fuels the desire to keep going.

It has spurred longevity and allowed me to see habits as a lifestyle of becoming, instead of a goalpost.

I started to keep a habit tracker as a way to measure my progress – I love the feeling of marking X's on a calendar template hung in my room as an indication of keeping to my habits for the day.

Pomodoro Technique

Game changer dedicated focus times with breaks in between to amplify concentration. There are apps and YouTube channels that are dedicated to this. The principle is to pick a task, set a timer for 25 – 30 mins (can be longer if you want) and work on set task until the timer is up. Take a 5 – 10 mins break and repeat. Once 4 slots are done, one can then enjoy a longer break. Repeat all over again!

I honestly couldn't believe how much work I could get done in a 25 – 30 mins dedicated time slot! Of course, with a lot of these, it's based on trial and error.

Consistency is key, but it hasn't been 100% every day. Consistency doesn't mean perfection but choosing to show up and try again day by day – that is my goal.

I have genuinely enjoyed learning about and applying all these so far. You know, those moments where you feel like you have some semblance of control for once in adulting? That's me on the days I successfully apply them.

16.

Health and Wellbeing

Mama took pride in looking after herself. From visits to the hairdressers, to getting her nails done, to buying Ankara fabrics to be sewn by some of the best tailors in our town. She had the best connects when it came to tailoring and they always had great bespoke designs. She would literally look like a wealthy Nigerian politician's wife whenever she wore them.

I really loved that about her. She took the time to look after herself. There was no excuse to looking unkept.

The older I get, the more I am becoming my mother's daughter in some ways. I too am beginning to take pride in looking after myself, not just outwardly but inwardly too.

I'm slowly learning about my body and how complex it is; what it can and cannot do, what body or skincare works well and what doesn't. I am learning about the role and impact of hormones on my mood and energy and how to navigate them; the list is endless. It is an interesting journey I didn't expect to go on, but I have found that it has come with the territory of getting older.

Although Mama did look after herself and encouraged me to do so (she taught me the basics such as washing myself, brushing my teeth and ironing my clothes), I've had to learn so much myself, experiment with all the knowledge and adapt certain things.

All of which has looked like researching and learning more about things like health supplements. I started taking multivitamins and probiotics to help with my gut. Apparently, taking care of your gut health is really good, and I have started to take foods and fruits high in fibre such as oats, kiwi, kidney beans, and broccoli in addition to the supplements. Trying to drink more water; the recommended 2-3L, making healthier food choices, being more active physically…you know, the usual cliché stuff…

Investing in dental care (being more intentional about visiting my dentist), trying to unplug from time to time and reduce my screen time, even though it is genuinely a struggle for me, trialling therapy, and learning more about the mind and mental health through books and podcasts.

Creating intentional time for Bible study, journaling, and prayer. It also looked like prioritising recovery including – rest, sleep, stretches, massages and facials.

Learning more about menstrual cycle and the effect on my mood, productivity and how I navigate my overall being during that 'time of the month.' It was interesting to discover how much all of this feeds into my day-to-day lifestyle. I have developed a newfound gratitude for the resources available to help women better understand their hormones and navigate their reproductive health.

I am genuinely thankful to whoever created the Flo app; it has been great and helpful for period-prediction and insight into understanding symptoms, experiences that come with my cycle, especially in moments where I may be in such a low mood, irritable or overly critical of myself. Moments where I am overly sensitive, easily triggered, or prone to cry every two seconds and wonder what in the world is wrong with me, only to realise that my period is due! Sigh…

It has been another reminder to give myself grace on this journey.

It can be hard trying to stay consistent with all of this. In those moments, I remind myself again that consistency does not mean perfection. The goal became to create a system which works and allows me to show up in the best way I know how to by the grace of God.

Another thing I had to learn and embrace for my wellbeing was how to seek and ask for help.

Mama can be going through the craziest, hardest, and hellish experiences of her life with a smile on her face. Carrying on with a brave face was her thing! She knew how to mask things well. An epiphany later, I realised that the apple really does not fall far from the tree. I, too, was no different. I *was* not the kind of person to shout about my issues. I just got on with them alone and found a way to brave them – a testament of Mama's genes and perhaps the Nigerian blood in me. Perhaps, a symptom also birthed from all the years of emotional neglect I experienced as a result of *japa* too.

I use the term *was,* because I refuse to let that be my portion still.

Strength. Resilience. The ability to carry things well are all great attributes. Ones that are usually applauded and should be. However, if counter dependency is the foundation, then it is neither healthy nor sustainable. I have definitely learnt that the hard way and still am.

I don't always have to be strong.

Why do I always feel the need to deal with things *well*? *Well* usually gave me no room to be weak or acknowledge the fact that things were crumbling. Sometimes, normalise being messy and bring dependable people into the mess.

Being messy: allowing your weakness and struggles to be seen, heard and felt in the moment. Not after it has been dealt with or polished, but, in the right here and right now. Giving the people close to me the opportunity to carry my burdens (the best way they can) too.

I don't have to carry everything on my own. I do not even have the capacity to; I am not God. Besides, I know God is real and He will help me. A lot of the times, He does this through people! So, I have started to normalise asking for help when needed and seek out space for my vulnerability to thrive.

This 'suffering in silence' ends with me. I can't have community yet carry things alone. It is not only a disservice to me, but to them too. That's why they are there. It does not always have to look pretty; life isn't.

Resilience is a great trait, but it does not have to be cultivated alone.

Adaora's Adulting Chronicles

From time to time, I have moments that remind me I am truly an adult when it comes to my health and wellbeing. The following conversation with Zara was one of them:

"You know you are now eligible for cervical screening?" Zara's voice mockingly echoed over the phone. I'm not sure why she felt I needed that reminder on the morning of my 25th birthday immediately after her heartfelt wishes, but I guess she was trying to be funny. She was not wrong though.

In the UK, females aged 25-49 are eligible for cervical screening and receive invitations every 3 years, by their General Practice (GP) [1]. Cervical screening is recommended as one of the best ways to protect women against cervical cancer. So, in this instance, I was due to be receiving my first invite soon.

As with most conditions, prevention is better than cure. Zara's comment reiterated the responsibility I had to my health and wellbeing. As well as the need to be committed to this as much as I can.

PART V

'Take home.'

17.

Lamentations: "It is Never-Ending"

In the first few weeks of getting my first car, I had the worst drive in a long while – stalled numerous of times at roundabouts or traffic lights and my lane positioning was out of the window. I even stalled in the middle of a particular roundabout and couldn't move off for a few good minutes; I had to put my hazard lights on.

It was embarrassing…

I got my first car over two years after my driver's licence, so my driving in general was a bit rusty. Many would argue that it was okay to be that rusty, especially after not driving for that long, but I was not one of the many. I didn't see it in that way. I felt so embarrassed, and really beat myself up about it.

As usual, I internalised those feelings for some time, but thank God for community – they didn't allow me to wallow in self-pity when it came to re-mastering this skill.

Day after day, I would challenge myself to go for a drive, especially after that incident.

I was reflecting on this experience and realised how I probably wouldn't have been a better driver if I hadn't gone through that terrible drive. The thing about my experience with the terrible drive was that by the end of it, I knew what I was doing wrong. I realised that each time I thought I selected the first gear to move off, I selected the third by accident, and because I hadn't driven for so long and was still getting used to the new car, I did not notice (that explained the numerous stalls!) Since then, I make sure to always select neutral, then first gear each time I move off.

I had to make those mistakes to learn better and grow confident in what not to do and what to do the next time. It's always from the mistakes or failures that we learn the most.

Adaora's Adulting Chronicles

A typology for adulting – rusty steps trying to navigate life, lots of mistakes, lots of learning, lots of unlearning and re-learning. Always something new to tackle, to figure out, to address. It is never ending.

For someone like me who does not like change, nor failing or making mistakes, this realisation can sometimes be hard to reconcile or accept. Learning to embrace this constant cycle of having to adapt has been a necessary wrestle.

"Wait till you have kids," one of my aunts once said during my regular laments about adulting. In that moment, I could not help but let out a very heavy sigh. A *you-mean-to-tell-me-it-gets-worse?* type sigh! I genuinely feel overwhelmed now and the journey is just beginning for me.

The truth is there is no blueprint. No manual per se. I am still figuring it out, and by the looks of it, everyone else is too and this remains constant – we are all navigating this in unique ways; in very different circumstances.

I must admit, this never-ending nature of adulting ~~feels~~ (is) exhausting at times. Most days, I genuinely feel like I cannot keep up. Other days, I feel as though it is impossible to keep up and adulting feels pretty unrealistic – how am I supposed to build and maintain my relationships, pay bills, unpack trauma, unlearn bad habits, build new and better habits, thrive at work, have fun, sleep well, eat well, manage my finances well, self-care, invest in myself spiritually, navigate the natural realities of life, look after my health and wellbeing, explore my passions, figure out my career, take care of Mama and Papa…all at the same time or in the space of an era?!

The ironic part of the list is that it is not exhaustive. It goes on and *even better*, evolves over time. It never ends…

Selah.

I feel the weight of adulting on the days; sometimes weeks that I have no capacity to engage with text messages, not necessarily because I do not *have* the time, but because I don't have the will to.

I feel the weight of adulting on the days where loneliness hits. The kind of loneliness that presents itself amidst company. Where the realisation that though I do have help on this journey, I have the responsibility on my shoulders and owe it to myself the benefit of trying.

I feel the weight of adulting in moments where it feels like I am doing so much, yet not enough, planting or at least trying to, but can't quite see the harvest yet…

I feel the weight of adulting on the days I'd wish to tell my younger self to slow down and not be in such a haste to grow up – "there's a season for everything Adaọra. Enjoy it while it is here."

I feel the weight of adulting in moments when it seems likes my mates are getting a hang of this phenomenon, whilst I am stuck in the shallows of **'still figuring it out.'**

I feel the weight of adulting some days, as a first greeting from social media. I know comparison is a thief of joy, but on those days, I let the thief in – willingly handing the keys over.

I feel the weight of adulting on the days where I have to figure things out – even on what to eat, and it seems like such a chore.

I feel the weight of adulting in moments where I struggle to let go of past hurts and make peace with the present.

I feel the weight of adulting on the days where it feels like my finances can never be enough for the growing list of responsibilities on my feeble back.

I feel the weight of adulting on the days I struggle with my mind.

Equally…

I feel the weight of adulting on the days I listen to my body and answer the call of rest.

I feel the weight of adulting on the days I choose to enjoy a longer shower and bask in the blessings of the mundane.

Adaora's Adulting Chronicles

I feel the weight of adulting on the days I choose to celebrate my wins, no matter how small.

I feel the weight of adulting on the times I chose to constantly remind myself of whose I am – God's very own. And although this journey might seem weighty and lonely, I have sustenance and help.

I feel the weight of adulting when I am held up by the hands of my community in encouragement, love and the gift of presence.

I feel the weight of adulting in moments I choose to acknowledge that there is in fact no blueprint per se. Therefore, I am on my own journey and nobody else's. My own timeline and nobody else's. This isn't a race; it is a marathon.

I feel the weight of adulting when I choose to see my mistakes as growth spurts. I did the best with what I knew and what I had. Without my mistakes, I would not have known better.

I feel the weight of adulting in moments where I begin to see brokenness in others too, even in the ones who hurt me the most – they too, need love.

I feel the weight of adulting in understanding that grace and patience is needed on this journey for myself and others.

I feel the weight of adulting in the many moments of realisations when I see the beauty and privilege it is to be there for Mama and Papa, in the capacity I can.

I feel the weight of adulting in choosing *surrender* as a lifestyle – surrender to the process, but most importantly, to the One who knows the beginning and the end: the Nazarene King. The One who carries and helps me as I navigate this journey…

18.

The Nazarene King

I was introduced to Him when I was younger. My family spoke of Him. Mama called on Him so many times. In lament, in confusion, in joy, in despair, in need; she called on Him.

She always spoke of the Power in His Name. She would tell of instances and stories where she witnessed this power in action. Even trivial scenarios where she tripped and almost physically fell, but because she called on His Name, she was immediately anchored mid-fall. She believed in Him that much!

She would tell tales of the countless moments He had come through for her. According to Mama, *e dey work.* Her faith in Him works.

As a result, I knew of Him, but if I'm honest, I didn't really *know* Him. Not until I was in my twenties.

University ushered me into this journey of *knowing* Him.

I had an identity crisis; a general apathy of life, of who I was and the faith I claimed to believe in. I also had an awakening – one which allowed me to see that I thought knowing of Him was the same as knowing Him; however, it was not.

I'm glad I embarked on this journey of knowing Him for myself.

Mama was right. He is indeed, an anchor. A strong and immovable one!

Some days, I ponder on how life can be a struggle, even with Him and wonder how I could have coped without Him. How would I have weathered through life without Him?

He literally carries me through life's many ebbs and flows. Just like He does, Mama.

Is it in those moments where He makes it clear that He *sees* me – like when

He gave Nkechi a dream about the solution to an issue I was facing at work that I did not share with anyone (not even Nkechi!), or was it on the days I broke down in tears on the floor as I felt His overwhelming love, or is it the growing nudges and impressions I get on what decisions to take that turn out to be the wisest in hindsight? Is it the strength and capacity to withstand stressful or hurtful situations, or the peace in many anxious moments? Is it the fact that I don't look like some of the *shege* I have been through!?

Or…is it the fact that I am a child? His child! Which gives me the freedom to put away the weightiness of adulting in surrender to a responsible Father who takes care of His own.

Adulting can be tough! Navigating life whilst trying to remain sane can be an extreme sport. However, I have come to realise it becomes easier with Him.

My faith has become a huge part of who I am. It is the core of who I am – the centre of my identity.

The Nazarene King is Jesus who is God.

Anytime I declare that I believe in Jesus, or say the Name ***Jesus***, there's almost an immediate feeling to defend the Name, or over-explain my rationale. Even worse, give some type of *disclaimer*.

Perhaps, it's because of the long-standing and growing cynicism against the Name and the faith. Some of which I guess is understandable but is not reflective of the faith in its purity.

Nevertheless, Mama, yet again was right: *e dey work!* I have known and I am on the continuous journey of knowing.

I believe in Jesus Christ. I believe that He is God.

He has been so pivotal in my adulting journey so far.

When all is said and done, I know that I am loved by the One who created the Heavens and the Earth – eternally. I know that nothing can separate me from this love. I know that I can rest in this love because it is not earned, but freely given by Him to me. To all, who believe in Him.

Therefore, regardless of what I achieve or don't achieve, I am enough in Him.

When push comes to shove, I know that He always leads and guides me. I've seen it firsthand.

Although I don't have all the answers to what my future would look like, I take solace that it will still be good because He is in it. No matter what that looks like.

Regardless of the things I have been through or might still be going through, I am enough and worthy because of Him. He says so, and I am His. What a blessed assurance that is!

Oh, what hope it brings to be loved and seen by the One who made all things – King, Father, Friend. Everything.

It is this hope that has kept me going, despite all the many things that have been and the many things that will be.

Knowing I have an anchor that transcends life itself. Knowing that although adulting means I am now responsible for myself, the ultimate responsibility for my life does not rest on me, but on Him. *The ultimate responsibility for my life is God's.* I can rest here...

I play my part and leave the rest to Him, *especially* the outcome. How relieving that is.

As one of Mama's favourite hymns puts it:

"From life's first cry to final breath, Jesus commands my destiny."

Glossary

Adaọra: The people's daughter. Name of Igbo descent. Typically for women

Ada: First daughter

Mama: Mother

Papa: Father

Ụwa emebiela ugbu a: The world has spoilt now

Adaego: daughter of wealth. Name of Igbo descent. Typically for women

Aunty*: a typical Nigerian way of showing respect to an older female, even though they might not be necessarily related to you.

NYSC: National Youth Service Corps

Nne, ọ ga adịnma: Daughter, all will be well

Japa: emigration. To emigrate

Oru Owerri festival: A festival and cultural carnival celebrated annually by the Igbo people of Owerri, in the Eastern part of Nigeria. A historical and cultural celebration of life, peace, love and unity [15]

Ezes: Kings

WAEC: West African Examinations Council

Agụ nwanyi: A lioness sort of. A woman who does everything including those that are exclusive reserves of men culturally. A woman that displays prowess in what she does. A strong woman as strong as a lion or Tigress. A smart woman

August meeting: An annual congress held by Igbo women in August

Pa: Father. Usually used for grandfathers. Synonym: Mpa

Obodo oyibo: Abroad

***E bere m akwa o*:** I cried o. A lament

Shege: A Nigerian term or slang used to describe extreme or unpleasant events, situations or circumstances. Hardship.

Obu: an outpost or small hut that is normally at the centre or entrance of a compound.

Ome udo: Peacemaker. A title

Reflective Piece

On upbringing and connecting the dots:

- What was my childhood like? What memories come to mind?
- In what ways has my upbringing shaped who I am today? Both good and bad?

On identity:

- Who am I?
- What is the foundation of my identity? Why is that? Is it sustainable?
- In what ways have I made the core of my identity something fickle?

On career:

- Do I struggle to champion my wins at work? How can I do better at that?
- How does my intersectionality show up at work?
- Can I receive constructive feedback?
- Am I attaching my worth to my work?
- What has been some of my biggest lessons since navigating the working world?

On success:

- How do I define success right now? Why is that success for me?

On boundaries:

- Do I have boundaries? Are they rigid or porous?
- Do my boundaries allow for some necessary inconvenience from time to time?

On friendships:

- Who do I consider a friend?
- Do I feel supported by my friends? Do I communicate my needs to them?

- What kind of friend am I? How can I be better?
- How is my attachment style and previous experiences showing up in my current friendships?

On conflicts:

- What is my response to conflict?
- Do I engage in healthy conflict?
- Does conflict feel like an attack on my person? If so, why?

On unpacking trauma:

- In what ways have previous experiences impacted the way I show up today?
- Was it trauma or was it just a negative experience?
- Am I ready for healing or am I still comfortable in the past?
- Am I pacing myself on this journey of navigating healing?
- What does healing look like?

On navigating romantic relationships:

- What do I want in a partner? By whose standard am I measuring my wants?
- Is this what I want or what I need?
- Will what I want or need in a partner matter in the long-term?

On productivity:

- What habits of mine are hindering my productivity?
- What habits can I implement to improve my productivity?

On health and wellbeing:

- What does self-care look like for me?
- Am I stewarding my body well?

On faith:

- What do I believe in? Why do I believe in it?
- Is it true?

References

1. **Cervical screening** - Cervical screening: programme overview - GOV.UK (www.gov.uk)

2. **What is an Overdraft?** | Overdraft Definition | NatWest

3. **Council Tax** | Who Pays Council Tax? | How Much Is Council Tax? | Mix (themix.org.uk)

4. **Council Tax**: what it is, what it costs and how to save money | MoneyHelper

5. **Student finance for undergraduates**: New full-time students - GOV.UK (www.gov.uk)

6. **Why first son is accorded high respect in Igboland** – Monarchs, Igbo leaders

7. **Repaying your student loan**: How much you repay - GOV.UK (www.gov.uk)

8. **About Us** | West Africa Examination Council Nigeria (waecnigeria.org)

9. **Think Like a White Man: Conquering the World** . . . While Black: Amazon.co.uk: Whytelaw III, Dr Boulé, Abbey, Nels: 9781786894342: Books

10. **Book**: Set Boundaries, find peace a guide to reclaiming yourself by Nedra Glover Tawwab

11. **APA Dictionary of Psychology**

12. **What is an Overdraft?** | Overdraft Definition | NatWest

13. **Council Tax** - Wikipedia

14. **Book: Why am I like this? How to break cycles, heal from trauma and restore your faith by Kobe Campbell**

15. **Oru Owerri Festival** | Historical And Cultural Celebration Of Life, Peace, Love And Unity Amongst Igbo People Of Owerri Municipal In Imo State, Nigeria | (www.metissagesanguemisto.com)

www.ingramcontent.com/pod-product-compliance
Lightning Source LLC
Chambersburg PA
CBHW031939090426
42811CB00002B/241
* 9 7 8 1 0 6 8 7 1 4 4 7 4 *